CONTENTS

INTRODUCTION

The Senate Committee on Finance has scheduled a public hearing on December 2, 2010, on "Tax Reform: Historical Trends in Income and Revenue." This document,[1] prepared by the staff of the Joint Committee on Taxation, provides a summary of the Federal tax system, briefly describes its historical development over the period of time beginning in 1975, and provides an appendix of selected historical data on Federal tax rates, Federal tax receipts, components of adjusted gross income, and other features of the Federal tax system.

The current Federal tax system has four main elements: (1) an income tax on individuals and corporations (which consist of both a "regular" income tax and an alternative minimum tax); (2) payroll taxes on wages (and corresponding taxes on self-employment income); (3) estate, gift, and generation-skipping transfer taxes, and (4) excise taxes on selected goods and services.

I. SUMMARY OF THE FEDERAL TAX SYSTEM

A. Individual Income Tax

In general

An income tax is imposed on individual citizens and residents of the United States.[2] The tax is based on an individual's taxable income. An individual computes his or her taxable income by reducing gross income by the sum of (i) the deductions allowable in computing adjusted gross income, (ii) the standard deduction (or itemized deductions, at the election of the taxpayer), and (iii) the deduction for personal exemptions. Graduated tax rates are then applied to a taxpayer's taxable income to determine his or her income tax liability. Lower rates apply to net capital gain and qualified dividend income. A taxpayer may also be subject to an alternative minimum tax. A taxpayer may reduce his or her income tax liability by certain tax credits. In the remainder of this section of the document, the broad structure of the individual income tax system is outlined, and certain parameters of the individual tax system are highlighted for selected years beginning with 1975.

Gross income

Gross income means "income from whatever source derived" other than certain items specifically excluded from gross income. Sources of gross income generally include, among other things, compensation for services, interest, dividends, capital gains, rents, royalties, alimony and separate maintenance payments, annuities, income from life insurance and endowment contracts (other than certain death benefits), pensions, gross profits from a trade or business, income in respect of a decedent, and income from S corporations, partnerships,[3] and trusts or estates.[4] Exclusions from gross income include death benefits payable under a life insurance contract, interest on certain tax-exempt State and local bonds, employer-provided health insurance, employer-provided pension contributions, and certain other employer-provided benefits.

---

[2] Foreign tax credits generally are available against U.S. income tax imposed on foreign source income to the extent of foreign income taxes paid on that income. A nonresident alien generally is subject to the U.S. individual income tax only on income with a sufficient nexus to the United States.

[3] In general, partnerships and S corporations are treated as pass-through entities for Federal income tax purposes. Thus, no Federal income tax is imposed at the entity level. Rather, income of these entities is passed through and taxed to the partners and shareholders.

[4] In general, estates and trusts (other than grantor trusts) pay an individual income tax on the taxable income of the estate or trust. Items of income which are distributed or required to be distributed under governing law or under the terms of the governing instrument generally are included in the income of the beneficiary and not the estate or trust. Estates and trusts determine their tax liability using a special tax rate schedule and may be subject to the alternative minimum tax. Certain trusts are treated as being owned by grantors in whole or in part for tax purposes; in such cases, the grantors are taxed on the income of the trust.

Adjusted gross income

An individual's adjusted gross income ("AGI") is determined by subtracting certain "above-the-line" deductions from gross income. These deductions include, among other things, trade or business expenses, losses from the sale or exchange of property, deductions attributable to rents and royalties, contributions to pensions and other retirement plans, certain moving expenses, and alimony payments.

Taxable income

In order to determine taxable income, an individual reduces AGI by any personal exemption deductions and either the applicable standard deduction or his or her itemized deductions. Personal exemptions generally are allowed for the taxpayer, his or her spouse, and any dependents. Table 1, below, summarizes the amount of personal exemptions for selected years between 1975 and 2010. Beginning in 1985, the amount of the personal exemption was indexed annually for inflation during the preceding year. Appendix Figure 1 shows the real value of the personal exemption from 1950 to 2010 in 2010 dollars.

**Table 1.–Personal Exemption and Standard Deduction,
Selected Calendar Years 1975-2010**

	1975	1985	1990	1995	2000	2005	2010
Personal Exemption	$750	$1,040	$2,050	$2,500	$2,800	$3,200	$3,650
Standard Deduction							
Single Individual	$1,600*	$2,390	$3,250	$3,900	$4,400	$5,000	$5,700
Head of Household	$1,600*	$2,390	$4,750	$5,750	$6,450	$7,300	$8,400
Married Couples Filing Jointly	$1,900*	$3,540	$5,450	$6,550	$7,350	$10,000	$11,400
Married Individual Filing Separately	$950*	$1,770	$2,725	$3,275	$3,675	$5,000	$5,700

* Shows minimum standard deduction.

A taxpayer may also reduce AGI by the amount of the applicable standard deduction. The basic standard deduction varies depending upon a taxpayer's filing status. Prior to 1977, the standard deduction was the larger of a "percentage standard deduction" and a "low-income allowance" (minimum standard deduction). The percentage standard deduction was a specific percentage of AGI, with a limit of a maximum standard deduction dollar amount. In 1975 that percentage was 16 percent, the maximum standard deduction was $2,300 for unmarried persons and heads of households and $2,600 for married taxpayers filing joint returns, and the minimum standard deduction was $1,600 for single returns and $1,900 for married taxpayers filing jointly. In 1977, a fixed dollar amount for the standard deduction was adopted by the Tax Reduction and Simplification Act of 1977 through introduction of "zero-bracket amount" exemption deductions. Those fixed dollar amounts have subsequently changed over time. Table 1, above, also shows the amount of standard deductions for the selected years. Also, an additional standard deduction is allowed with respect to any individual who is elderly or blind.[5]

In lieu of taking the applicable standard deduction, an individual may elect to itemize deductions. The deductions that may be itemized include State and local income taxes (or, in lieu of income, sales)[6], real property and certain personal property taxes, home mortgage interest, charitable contributions, certain investment interest, medical expenses (in excess of 7.5 percent of AGI), casualty and theft losses (in excess of 10 percent of AGI and in excess of $100 per loss), and certain miscellaneous expenses (in excess of two percent of AGI). Generally, the total amount of most itemized deductions allowed is reduced for taxpayers with incomes over a certain threshold amount, which is indexed annually for inflation. Appendix Table 1 shows the number and percent of returns claiming the standard deduction versus itemizing deduction from 1950 to 2008. Appendix Figure 2 shows the real value of the standard deduction for single filers and married filers filing jointly from 1970 to 2010, and the percentage taking the standard deduction.

In recent decades there have been many changes to the individual income tax base. The increased availability of Individual Retirement Arrangements[7] (commonly called ("IRAs")) followed by the subsequent curtailment of their availability[8] and the taxation of a portion of Social Security and Railroad Retirement Tier 1 benefits[9] are two items which affect the measurement of gross income for some taxpayers. The enactment of "pre-tax benefits" designed to respond to increased health-care costs are examples of changes to adjusted gross income.[10] The calculation of taxable income has been affected by the numerous changes to itemized deductions. Examples of such changes include the creation of the two-percent floor on miscellaneous itemized deductions,[11] changes to the tax treatment of moving expenses,[12] and

---

[5] For 2010, the additional amount is $1,100 for married taxpayers (for each spouse meeting the applicable criterion) and surviving spouses. The additional amount for single individuals and heads of households is $1,400. If an individual is both blind and aged, the individual is entitled to two additional standard deductions, for a total additional amount (for 2010) of $2,200 or $2,800, as applicable.

[6] Itemized deductions for State and local income taxes expire at the end of 2010.

[7] The Economic Recovery Tax Act of 1981 (Pub. L. No. 97-34).

[8] The Tax Reform Act of 1986 (Pub. L. No. 99-514).

[9] The Social Security Amendments of 1983 (Pub. L. No. 98-21), as amended by the Railroad Retirement Solvency Act of 1983 (Pub. L. No. 98-76) and the Consolidated Budget Reconciliation Act of 1985 (Pub. L. No. 99-272). The Omnibus Budget Reconciliation Act of 1993 (Pub. L. No. 103-66).

[10] The Revenue Act of 1978 (Pub. L. No. 95-600).

[11] The Tax Reform Act of 1986 (Pub. L. No. 99-514).

[12] The Omnibus Budget Reconciliation Act of 1993 (Pub. L. No. 103-66).

changes to the floor on the itemized deduction for medical expenses.[13] Another significant change to the individual income tax base was the enactment of a limitation on passive losses which affects tax liability on certain business investments by individuals.[14]

Tax liability

In general

A taxpayer's net income tax liability is the greater of (1) regular individual income tax liability reduced by credits allowed against the regular tax, or (2) tentative minimum tax reduced by credits allowed against the minimum tax.

Regular tax liability

To determine regular tax liability, a taxpayer generally must apply the tax rate schedules (or the tax tables) to his or her regular taxable income. The rate schedules are broken into several ranges of income, known as income brackets, and the marginal tax rate increases as a taxpayer's income increases. Separate rate schedules apply based on an individual's filing status. The regular individual income tax rate schedules for 1975, 1985, 1990, 1995, 2000, and the present year 2010 are shown in Appendix Tables 2 through 7.

Figure 1 below, shows the top tax bracket rate and income level at which it begins to apply for married tax payers filing jointly for selected years. Figure 2 shows the bottom rate and the income level at which it would begin to apply for married taxpayers filing jointly, calculated as the sum of the standard deduction and two personal exemptions. Appendix Figure 3 shows the full rate structure for selected years in real 2010 dollars.

---

[13] The Internal Revenue Act of 1954 (Pub. L. No. 83-59) set the floor at 3%, the 1982 Tax and Equity Fiscal Responsibility Act (Pub. L. No. 97-248) raised the floor to 5%, the Tax Reform Act of 1986 (Pub. L. No. 99-514) raised the floor to 7.5%, and the Patient Protection and Affordable Care Act (Pub. L. No. 111-148) raised the floor to 10%.

[14] A more complete discussion of the passive loss rules is included in the corporate income tax section of this pamphlet.

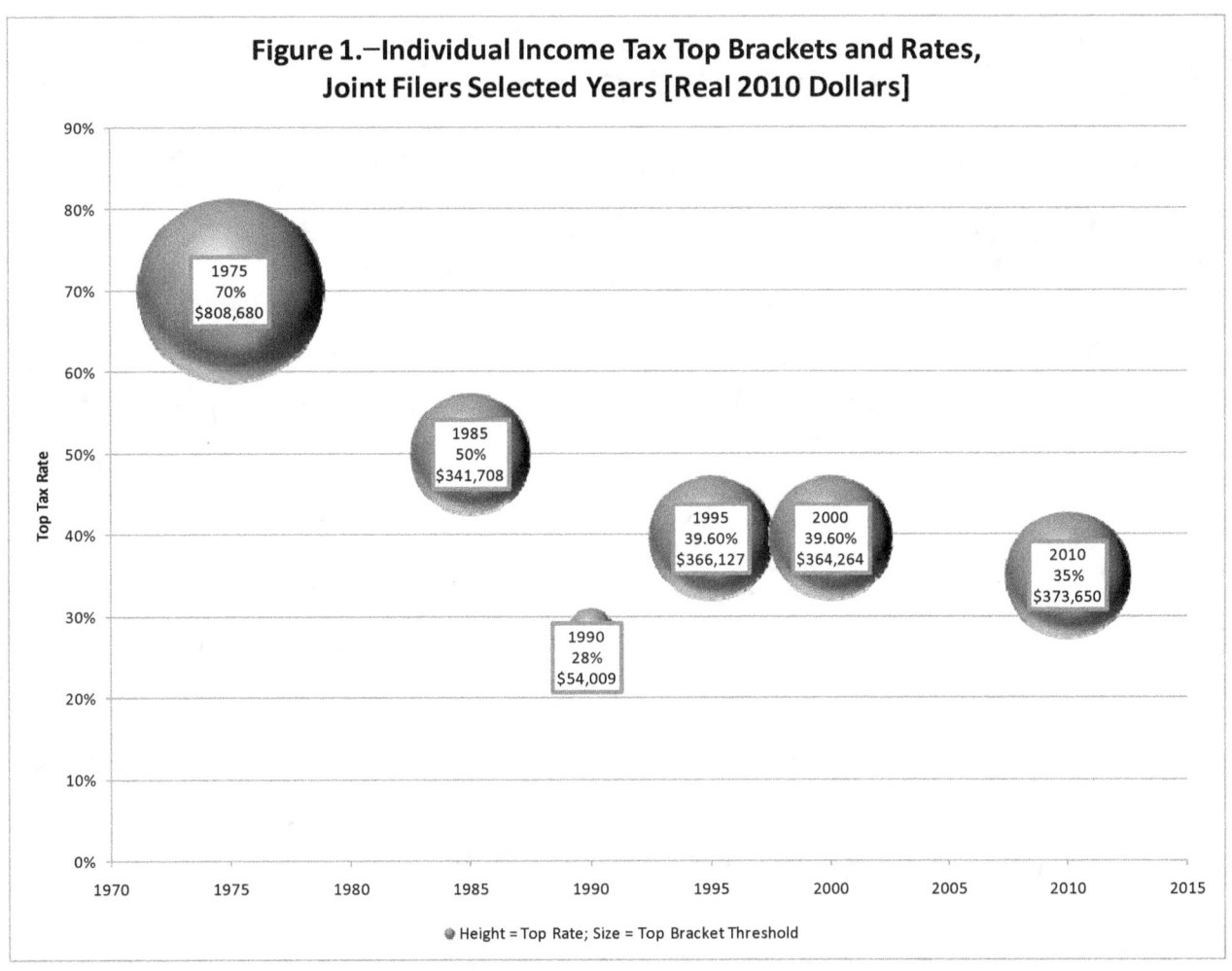

Figure 1.–Individual Income Tax Top Brackets and Rates, Joint Filers Selected Years [Real 2010 Dollars]

● Height = Top Rate; Size = Top Bracket Threshold

Special rules have long applied to capital gain income to limit the amount of gain included in income or to reduce the rate of tax imposed on gain. Appendix Table 8 summarizes the tax regime for long-term capital gain from 1913 to 2010.

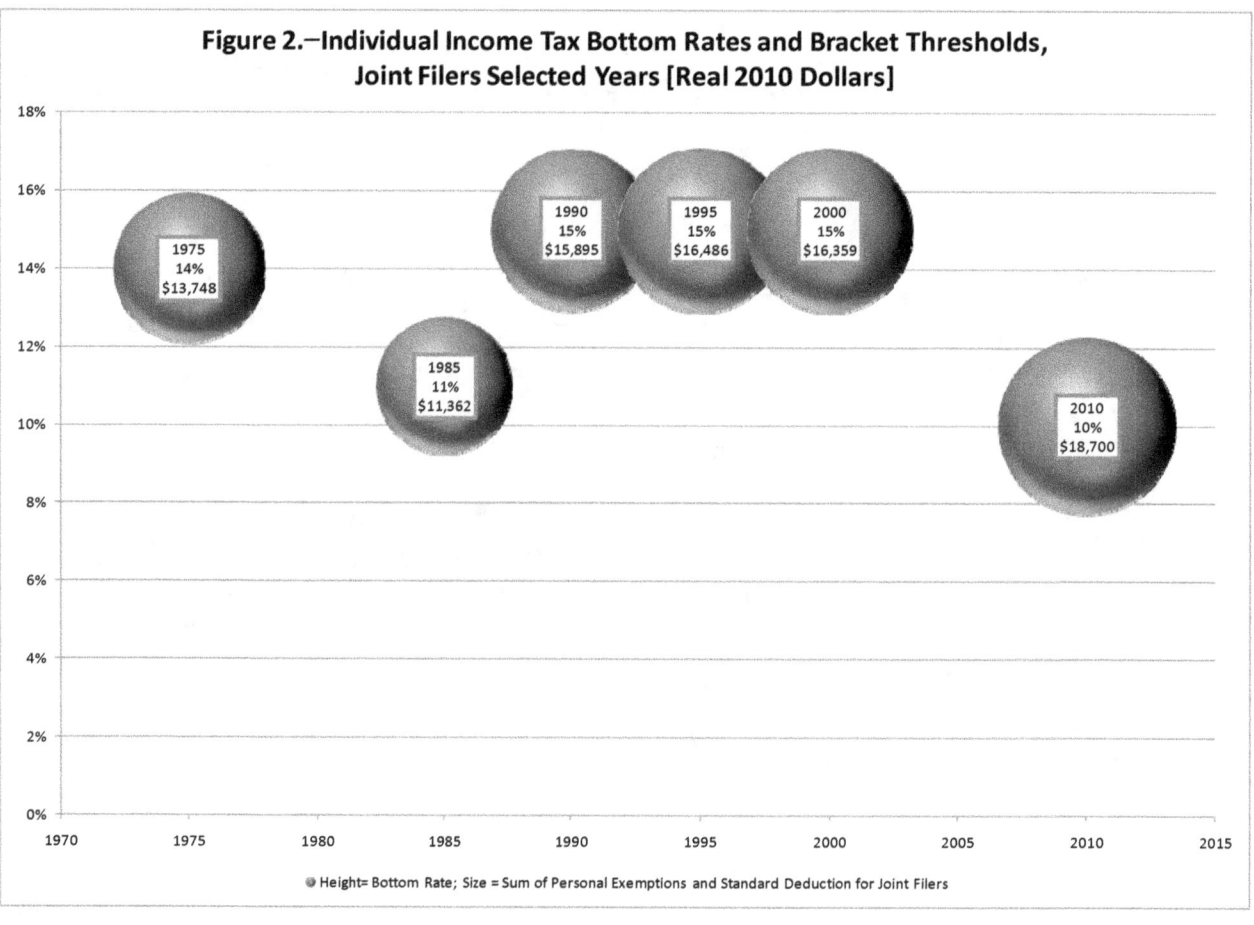

Figure 2.–Individual Income Tax Bottom Rates and Bracket Thresholds, Joint Filers Selected Years [Real 2010 Dollars]

◉ Height= Bottom Rate; Size = Sum of Personal Exemptions and Standard Deduction for Joint Filers

Tax credits

In general.–The individual may reduce his or her tax liability by any available tax credits. Tax credits are allowed for certain business expenditures, certain foreign income taxes paid or accrued, certain dependent children and child care expenditures, and for certain elderly or disabled individuals. In addition, a refundable earned income tax credit ("EITC") is available to low-income workers who satisfy certain requirements.

A brief description of the most widely used credits follows.

Earned income tax credit.–The EITC, enacted in 1975, generally equals a specified percentage of wages up to a maximum credit amount. The maximum credit amount applies over a certain income range and then diminishes to zero over a certain income range. The income ranges and credit percentages have been revised several times since enactment, expanding the credit. As originally enacted in 1975, the credit was 10 percent of the first $4,000 of earned income[15] (i.e., a maximum credit of $400). The credit began to be phased out for filing units

---

[15] Earned income is defined as the sum of wages, salaries, tips, and other taxable employee compensation plus net self-employment earnings.

with earned income (or AGI, if greater) above $4,000, and was entirely phased out for filing units with income of $8,000.

The Revenue Act of 1978 increased the maximum EITC to $500 and the income level at which the phaseout began was raised to $6,000. The Deficit Reduction Act of 1984 increased the maximum EITC to $550 (11 percent of the first $5,000 of earned income) and the credit was phased out beginning at $6,500 of income and ending at $11,000. Similarly in 1985, the credit was 14 percent of the first $5,000 of earned income and the maximum EITC was $550, while the credit began to be phased out for filing units with earned income above $6,500 and was entirely phased out for filing units with income of $11,000.

The Tax Reform Act of 1986 increased the maximum EITC to $800 (14 percent of the first $5,714 of earned income), beginning in 1987. The maximum credit was reduced by 10 cents for each dollar of earned income (or AGI, if greater) in excess of $9,000 ($6,500 in 1987). These $5,714 and $9,000 amounts (stated above in 1985 dollars) were indexed for inflation.

In 1990 and again in 1993, Congress enacted substantial expansions of the EITC. The Omnibus Budget Reconciliation Act of 1990 substantially increased the maximum amount of the credit. In 1990, the credit rate was 14 percent of the first $6,810 of earned income and the maximum EITC was $953. The credit was phased out beginning at $10,730 in income and ending at $20,264. The Omnibus Budget Reconciliation Act of 1993 expanded the credit in several ways. For individuals with one qualifying child, the credit was increased to 26.3 percent of the first $7,750 of earned income in 1994. For 1995 and thereafter, the credit rate was increased to 34 percent. Therefore in 1995, the credit was 34 percent of the first $6,160 of the earned income (this is a $6,000 base in 1994, adjusted for inflation), and the phaseout rate was 15.98 percent. The maximum credit for individuals with one qualifying child in 1995 was $2,094. For individuals with two or more qualifying children, the credit was increased to 36 percent of the first $8,640 of earned income in 1995. The maximum credit for individuals with two or more qualifying children in 1995 was $3,110 and was reduced by 20.22 percent of earned income (or AGI, if greater) in excess of $11,290. As for individuals with no children, the maximum credit was $314.

As seen above, the amount of the EITC varies depending upon the taxpayer's earned income and whether the taxpayer has one, more than one, or no qualifying children. In 2000, the maximum EITC was $3,888 for taxpayers with more than two qualifying children, $2,353 for taxpayers with one qualifying child, and $353 for taxpayers with no qualifying children. For 2000, the phase-out range was $5,770 to $10,380 for no qualifying children, $12,690 to $27,415 for one qualifying child, and $12,690 to $31,152 for two or more qualifying children.

In 2010, the maximum EITC is $5,666 for taxpayers with more than two qualifying children, $5,036 for taxpayers with two qualifying children, $3,050 for taxpayers with one qualifying child, and $457 for taxpayers with no qualifying children. Also, the EITC is phased out along certain phase-out ranges. In 2010, the phase-out range is $7,480 to $13,460 for no qualifying children, $16,450 to $35,535 for one qualifying child, $16,450 to $40,363 for two qualifying children, and $16,450 to $43,352 for three or more qualifying children. Also for 2010, the phase-out threshold for married couples filing a joint return is increased by $5,010.

Appendix Table 9 shows the number of recipients of the EITC and the average amount of the credit from 1975 to 2008.

Child tax credit.–Before 1997, taxpayers could not claim tax credits based solely on the number of dependent children. Instead, they were generally able to claim a personal exemption for each of these dependents. The Taxpayer Relief Act of 1997 provided for a $500 ($400 for taxable year 1998) tax credit for each qualifying child under the age of 17 while retaining the personal exemption rules. A qualifying child is defined as an individual for whom the taxpayer can claim a dependency exemption and who is a son or daughter of the taxpayer (or a descendant of either), a stepson or stepdaughter of the taxpayer, or an eligible foster child of the taxpayer. For taxpayers with modified AGI in excess of certain thresholds, the child credit is phased out. The phase out rate is $50 for each $1,000 of modified AGI[16] (or a fraction thereof) in excess of the threshold. For married taxpayers filing joint returns, the threshold is $110,000. For taxpayers filing single or head of household returns, the threshold is $75,000. For married taxpayers filing separate returns, the threshold is $55,000. These thresholds are not indexed for inflation.

The Economic Growth and Tax Relief Reconciliation Act of 2001 ("EGTRRA") increased the child credit on a phased in basis, reaching $1,000 in 2011, and provided for limited refundability of the credit.[17] EGTRRA made the child tax credit refundable to the extent of 10 percent of the taxpayer's earned income in excess of $10,000 for calendar years 2001-2004. The percentage was scheduled to increase to 15 percent for calendar years 2005 and thereafter. The $10,000 amount was indexed for inflation beginning in 2002. Families with three of more children were allowed a refundable credit for the amount by which the taxpayer's social security taxes exceed the taxpayer's earned income credit, if that amount is greater than the refundable credit based on the taxpayer's earned income in excess of $10,000. EGTRRA also provided that the refundable portion of the child tax credit does not constitute income and shall not be treated as resources for purposes of determining eligibility or the amount or nature of benefits or assistance under any Federal program or any State or local program financed with Federal Funds.

The Job Creation and Growth Tax Relief Reconciliation Act of 2003 ("JGTRRA") increased the amount of the child tax credit from $600 to $1,000 for 2003 and 2004.[18]

The credit is allowable against the regular tax and, for taxable years beginning before January 1, 2011, is allowed against the AMT. To the extent the child tax credit exceeds the

---

[16] For these purposes modified AGI is computed by increasing the taxpayer's AGI by the amount otherwise excluded under Code sections 911, 931, and 933 (relating to the exclusion of income of U.S. citizens or residents living abroad; residents of Guam, American Samoa, and the Northern Marina Islands; and residents of Puerto Rico, respectively).

[17] The credit reverts to $500, and all of the other EGTRRA child tax credit rules expire, for taxable years beginning after December 31, 2010, under the sunset provision of EGTRRA.

[18] The Working Families Tax Relief Act of 2004 increased the child tax credit to $1,000 for 2005-2009 and accelerated to 2004 the refundability of the credit to 15 percent of earned income in excess of $10,750, with indexing.

taxpayer's tax liability, the taxpayer is eligible for a refundable credit (the additional child tax credit) equal to 15 percent of earned income in excess of a threshold dollar amount (the "earned income" formula). EGTRRA provided, in general, that this threshold dollar amount is $10,000 indexed for inflation from 2001. The American Recovery and Reinvestment Act of 2009 set the threshold at $3,000 for both 2009 and 2010. Accordingly, for 2010, the child tax credit generally is $1,000 but is phased-out for individuals with income over certain thresholds. For 2010, the child tax credit is refundable up to the greater of: (1) 15 percent of the taxpayer's earned income in excess of $3,000; or (2) for families with three or more children, the amount by which the taxpayer's social security taxes exceed the taxpayer's earned income.

Making work pay tax credit.–The making work pay credit is a temporary refundable income tax credit available to eligible individuals for two years (taxable years beginning in 2009 and 2010).

The credit is the lesser of: (1) 6.2 percent of an individual's earned income; or (2) $400 ($800 in the case of a joint return). For purposes of calculating an eligible individual's credit, the definition of earned income is the same as for the earned income tax credit with two modifications. First, earned income does not include net earnings from self-employment which are not taken into account in computing taxable income. Second, earned income includes combat pay excluded from gross income under section 112.

The credit is phased out at a rate of two percent of the eligible individual's modified adjusted gross income above $75,000 ($150,000 in the case of a joint return). For purposes of the phase-out, an eligible individual's modified adjusted gross income is the eligible individual's adjusted gross income increased by any amount excluded from gross income under sections 911, 931, or 933. An eligible individual is any individual other than: (1) a nonresident alien; (2) an individual with respect to whom another individual may claim a dependency deduction for a taxable year beginning in a calendar year in which the eligible individual's taxable year begins; and (3) an estate or trust.

Alternative minimum tax liability

In general

An alternative minimum tax is imposed on an individual, estate, or trust in an amount by which the tentative minimum tax exceeds the regular income tax for the taxable year. The tentative minimum tax is the sum of (1) 26 percent of so much of the taxable excess as does not exceed $175,000 ($87,500 in the case of a married individual filing a separate return) and (2) 28 percent of the remaining taxable excess. The taxable excess is so much of the alternative minimum taxable income ("AMTI") as exceeds the exemption amount. The maximum tax rates on net capital gain and dividends used in computing the regular tax are also used in computing the tentative minimum tax. AMTI is the taxpayer's taxable income increased by the taxpayer's "tax preference items" and adjusted by redetermining the tax treatment of certain items in a manner that negates the deferral of income resulting from the regular tax treatment of those items.

The exemption amounts for 2010 are: (1) $45,000 in the case of married individuals filing a joint return and surviving spouses; (2) $33,750 in the case of unmarried individuals other than surviving spouses; (3) $22,500 in the case of married individuals filing separate returns; and (4) $22,500 in the case of an estate or trust.[19] The exemption amounts are phased out by an amount equal to 25 percent of the amount by which the individual's AMTI exceeds: (1) $150,000 in the case of married individuals filing a joint return and surviving spouses; (2) $112,500 in the case of other unmarried individuals; and (3) $75,000 in the case of married individuals filing separate returns or an estate or a trust. These amounts are not indexed for inflation.

Among the preferences and adjustments applicable to the individual alternative minimum tax are accelerated depreciation on certain property used in a trade or business, circulation expenditures, research and experimental expenditures, certain expenses and allowances related to oil and gas and mining exploration and development, certain tax-exempt interest income, and a portion of the amount of gain excluded with respect to the sale or disposition of certain small business stock. In addition, personal exemptions, the standard deduction, and certain itemized deductions, such as State and local taxes and miscellaneous deductions items, are not allowed to reduce alternative minimum taxable income.

<u>Legislative history</u>

The Tax Equity and Fiscal Responsibility Act of 1982 enacted the first comprehensive individual AMT.[20] Under the 1982 Act, in computing AMTI, the deduction for State and local taxes, the deduction for personal exemptions, the standard deduction, and the deduction for interest on home equity loans were not allowed. Incentive stock option gain was included in AMTI. These remain the principal preferences and adjustments under present law.

The Tax Reform Act of 1986 largely retained the structure of the prior-law AMT, since 1986, several changes have been made to the computation of the individual AMT. The principal changes are set forth below:

<u>Adjustments and preferences</u>.–The principal changes made in the determination of AMTI were to repeal the preference for charitable contributions of appreciated property; repeal the preference for percentage depletion on oil and gas wells; substantially reduce the amount of the preference for intangible drilling expenses; and repeal the requirement that alternative depreciation lives be used in computing the deduction for ACRS depreciation.

<u>Rates</u>.–The Omnibus Budget Reconciliation Act of 1990 increased the individual AMT tax rate from 21 percent to 24 and the rate was further increased by the Omnibus Budget

---

[19] The exemption amounts for 2009 were: (1) $70,950 in the case of married individuals filing a joint return and surviving spouses; (2) $46,700 in the case of unmarried individuals other than surviving spouses; (3) $35,475 in the case of married individuals filing separate returns; and (4) $35,475 in the case of an estate or trust.

[20] An add-on minimum tax was first enacted by the Tax Reform Act of 1969. The add-on minimum tax was repealed by the 1982 Act. The add-on minimum tax, as originally enacted, generally was a tax at a 10-percent rate on the sum of the specified tax preferences in excess of the sum of $30,000 plus the taxpayer's regular tax.

Reconciliation Act of 1993 to the 26- and 28-percent rate structure of present law (when the maximum regular tax rate was increased from 31 percent to 39.6 percent).

Exemption amounts.–The Omnibus Budget Reconciliation Act of 1993 increased the AMT exemption amounts to $45,000 ($33,750 for unmarried taxpayers). The AMT exemption amounts were temporarily increased to $49,000 ($35,750 for unmarried individuals) for 2001 and 2002, to $58,000 ($40,250 for unmarried individuals) for 2003, 2004, and 2005, to $62,550 ($42,500 for unmarried individuals) for 2006, $66,250 ($44,350 for unmarried individuals) in 2007, $69,950 ($46,200 for unmarried individuals) in 2008, and to $70,950 ($46,700 for unmarried individuals) in 2009.

Credits.–For 1998 and subsequent years, the nonrefundable personal credits have been allowed on a temporary basis to offset the AMT. The last extension, through 2009, was enacted by the American Recovery and Reinvestment Act of 2009.

B. Employment Taxes

Social security benefits and certain Medicare benefits are financed primarily by payroll taxes on covered wages. The Federal Insurance Contributions Act ("FICA") imposes a tax on employers based on the amount of wages paid to an employee during the year. The tax as imposed in 1975 was composed of two parts: (1) the old age, survivors, and disability insurance ("OASDI") tax equal to 5.85 percent of covered wages up to the taxable wage base of $14,100; and (2) the Medicare hospital insurance ("HI") tax amount equal to 0.9 percent of covered wages. In addition to the tax on employers, each employee is subject to FICA taxes equal to the amount of tax imposed on the employer. The employee tax generally must be withheld and remitted to the Federal government by the employer.[21] Self-employed taxpayers are subject to payroll tax under the Self-Employed Contributions Act ("SECA"). The SECA tax in 1975 was imposed on the same wage base and was composed of the same OASDI and HI components, but the rate was equal to 7.9 percent (7 percent OASDI, 0.9 percent HI).

The earnings base is indexed each year automatically according to a statutory formula. Any increase in the earnings base is based on the increase in average wages in the economy.[22]

FICA payroll taxes were modified by the Social Security Amendments of 1983 (the "1983 Act").[23] Under this Act, coverage was extended on a compulsory basis to Federal employees,[24] members of Congress, the President and Vice-President, Federal judges, and employees of non-profit organizations. Up to half of the OASDI benefits were made includable in taxable income for taxpayers with incomes above certain base amounts. The 1983 Act also accelerated a previously-enacted increase in the tax rate and raised the retirement age, to begin in 2000.

The 1983 Act also raised SECA payroll taxes considerably. Prior to the 1983 Act, SECA taxes had been deliberately set lower than FICA taxes. The 1983 Act sought to erase this discrepancy starting in 1984 and achieving parity between SECA and FICA by 1990. Therefore, effective in 1990, only 92.35 percent of covered wages are taxable as "net earnings from self-

---

[21] The OASDI and HI payroll tax is generally collected as a single tax with portions of it allocated by statute among three separate trust funds (OASI, DI and HI).

[22] The earnings base can only increase in a year in which there was an increase in benefits under the cost-of-living adjustment (COLA) formula. If there was no increase in benefits, the earnings base is prohibited from increasing. Sec. 230(a) of the Social Security Act. Since there was no increase in benefits from 2009 through 2011, the earnings base remained constant from 2009 through 2011 too.

[23] Pub. L. No. 98-2. High unemployment rates throughout the 70s as well as a decrease in real wages led to fears that the system would be vastly underfunded and a need to generate revenue quickly. The National Commission on Social Security Reform was created to address the issue, and its final report formed the basis for many of the 1983 amendments.

[24] If hired after December 31, 1983.

employment"[25] and the self-employed taxpayer receives a deduction for 50 percent of SECA taxes paid.[26]

The Omnibus Budget Reconciliation Act of 1989 modified the formula under which the annual increase in the earnings base is calculated. The modification included in the formula certain types of deferred compensation, such as contributions to a 401(k) plan.

As a result of the Omnibus Budget Reconciliation Act of 1990[27] the HI base was raised to $125,000 in 1992 and $135,000 in 1993.

As part of the Omnibus Budget Reconciliation Act of 1993,[28] the earnings base for the HI portion of the tax was removed, making all earnings taxable for HI purposes, effective in 1994. The maximum portion of social security benefits includable in taxable income was raised from up to half, to up to 85 percent, and the ceilings on the relevant income thresholds were increased.

Table 2 below, shows the evolution of the taxable wage base and rates of tax since 1975.

---

[25] This adjustment is made to reflect the fact that employees do not pay FICA taxes on the employer's portion of the FICA tax. Thus, the base is reduced by 7.65 percent, the employer's share of FICA taxes.

[26] This deduction mirrors the treatment for employees, who do not pay income tax on the employer's portion of the FICA tax.

[27] Pub. L. No. 101-518.

[28] Pub. L. No. 103-66.

Table 2.–Social Insurance Taxable Wage Base and Rates of Tax

Year	Annual Maximum Taxable Earnings	Contribution Rate for Employers and Employees (Percent of Covered Earnings)				Contribution Rate for Self-Employed Persons		
		Total	OASI	DI	HI	Total	OASDI	HI
1975	$14,100	5.85	4.375	0.575	0.9	7.9	7.0	0.9
1976	$15,300	5.85	4.375	0.575	0.9	7.9	7.0	0.9
1977	$16,500	5.85	4.375	0.575	0.9	7.9	7.0	0.9
1978	$17,700	6.05	4.275	0.775	1.00	8.1	7.1	1.0
1979	$22,900	6.13	4.33	0.75	1.05	8.1	7.05	1.05
1980	$25,900	6.13	4.52	0.56	1.05	8.1	7.05	1.05
1981	$29,700	6.65	4.70	0.65	1.3	9.3	8.0	1.3
1982	$32,400	6.7	4.575	0.825	1.3	9.35	8.05	1.3
1983	$35,700	6.7	4.775	0.625	1.3	9.35	8.05	1.3
1984[1]	$37,800	7.0	5.2	0.5	1.3	14.00	11.4	2.6
1985	$39,600	7.05	5.2	0.5	1.35	14.10	11.4	2.7
1986	$42,000	7.15	5.2	0.5	1.45	14.30	11.4	2.9
1987	$43,800	7.15	5.2	0.5	1.45	14.30	11.4	2.9
1988	$45,000	7.51	5.53	0.53	1.45	15.02	12.12	2.9
1989	$48,000	7.51	5.53	0.53	1.45	15.02	12.12	2.9
1990	$51,300	7.65	5.6	0.6	1.45	15.3	12.4	2.9
1991	$53,400	7.65	5.6	0.6	1.45	15.3	12.4	2.9
1992	$55,500	7.65	5.6	0.6	1.45	15.3	12.4	2.9
1993	$57,600	7.65	5.6	0.6	1.45	15.3	12.4	2.9
1994	$60,600	7.65	5.26	0.94	1.45	15.3	12.4	2.9
1995	$61,200	7.65	5.26	0.94	1.45	15.3	12.4	2.9
1996	$62,700	7.65	5.26	0.94	1.45	15.3	12.4	2.9
1997	$65,400	7.65	5.35	0.85	1.45	15.3	12.4	2.9
1998	$68,400	7.65	5.35	0.85	1.45	15.3	12.4	2.9
1999	$72,600	7.65	5.35	0.85	1.45	15.3	12.4	2.9
2000	$76,200	7.65	5.3	0.9	1.45	15.3	12.4	2.9
2001	$80,400	7.65	5.3	0.9	1.45	15.3	12.4	2.9
2002	$84,900	7.65	5.3	0.9	1.45	15.3	12.4	2.9
2003	$87,900	7.65	5.3	0.9	1.45	15.3	12.4	2.9
2004	$87,900	7.65	5.3	0.9	1.45	15.3	12.4	2.9
2005	$90,000	7.65	5.3	0.9	1.45	15.3	12.4	2.9
2006	$94,200	7.65	5.3	0.9	1.45	15.3	12.4	2.9
2007	$97,500	7.65	5.3	0.9	1.45	15.3	12.4	2.9
2008	$102,000	7.65	5.3	0.9	1.45	15.3	12.4	2.9
2009	$106,800	7.65	5.3	0.9	1.45	15.3	12.4	2.9
2010	$106,800	7.65	5.3	0.9	1.45	15.3	12.4	2.9

[1] For 1984 only, employees were allowed a credit of .3 percent of taxable wages against their FICA tax liability, reducing the effective rate to 6.7 percent.

C. Corporate Income Tax

Since its inception in 1909, the Federal income tax assessed on the earnings of corporations as entities separate and apart from their owners has undergone significant changes, both with respect to the corporate income tax rate structure and the tax base. The following will describe the corporate income tax in general as it exists today, a history of the corporate income tax rates since 1975, and certain significant changes to the corporate income tax base since 1975.

In general

Corporations organized under the laws of any of the 50 States (and the District of Columbia) generally are subject to the U.S. corporate income tax on their worldwide taxable income.[29]

The taxable income of a corporation generally is comprised of gross income less allowable deductions. Gross income generally is income derived from any source, including gross profit from the sale of goods and services to customers, rents, royalties, interest (other than interest from certain indebtedness issued by State and local governments), dividends, gains from the sale of business and investment assets, and other income.

Allowable deductions include ordinary and necessary business expenses, such as salaries, wages, contributions to profit-sharing and pension plans and other employee benefit programs, repairs, bad debts, taxes (other than Federal income taxes), contributions to charitable organizations (subject to an income limitation), advertising, interest expense, certain losses, selling expenses, and other expenses. Expenditures that produce benefits in future taxable years to a taxpayer's business or income-producing activities (such as the purchase of plant and equipment) generally are capitalized and recovered over time through depreciation, amortization or depletion allowances. A net operating loss incurred in one taxable year typically may be carried back two years or carried forward 20 years and allowed as a deduction in another taxable year. Deductions are also allowed for certain amounts despite the lack of a direct expenditure by the taxpayer. For example, a deduction is allowed for all or a portion of the amount of dividends received by a corporation from another corporation (provided certain ownership requirements are satisfied). Moreover, a deduction is allowed for a portion of the amount of income attributable to certain manufacturing activities.

The Code also specifies certain expenditures that typically may not be deducted, such as expenses associated with earning tax-exempt income,[30] certain entertainment expenditures,

---

[29] Foreign tax credits generally are available against U.S. income tax imposed on foreign source income to the extent of foreign income taxes paid on that income. A foreign corporation generally is subject to the U.S. corporate income tax only on income with a sufficient nexus to the United States.

A qualified small business corporation may elect, under subchapter S of the Code, not to be subject to the corporate income tax. If an S corporation election is made, the income of the corporation will flow through to the shareholders and be taxable directly to the shareholders. Special rules (not discussed herein) also apply to a corporation that has elected to be taxable as a regulated investment company (RIC), real estate investment trust (REIT), or real estate mortgage investment conduit (REMIC).

certain executive compensation in excess of $1,000,000 per year, a portion of the interest on certain high-yield debt obligations that resemble equity, and fines, penalties, bribes, kickbacks and illegal payments.

In contrast to the treatment of capital gains in the individual income tax, no separate rate structure exists for corporate capital gains. Thus, the maximum rate of tax on the net capital gains of a corporation is 35 percent. A corporation may not deduct the amount of capital losses in excess of capital gains for any taxable year. Disallowed capital losses may be carried back three years or carried forward five years.

Corporations are taxed at lower rates on income from certain domestic production activities. This rate reduction is effected by the allowance of a deduction equal to a percentage of qualifying domestic production activities income. For taxable years beginning in 2008 and 2009, the deduction is equal to six percent of the income from manufacturing, construction, and certain other activities specified in the Code. Beginning in 2010, the percentage is increased to nine percent.[31]

Like individuals, corporations may reduce their tax liability by any applicable tax credits. Tax credits applicable to businesses include, but are not limited to, credits for producing fuels from nonconventional sources, investment tax credits (applicable to investment in certain renewable energy property and the rehabilitation of certain real property), the alcohol fuels credit (applicable to production of certain alcohol fuels), the research credit (applicable to qualified research expenses incurred prior to December 31, 2009), the low-income housing credit (applicable to investment in certain low-income housing projects), the enhanced oil recovery credit (applicable to the recovery of certain difficult-to-extract oil reserves), the empowerment zone employment credit (applicable to wages paid to certain residents of or employees in empowerment zones), the work opportunity credit (applicable to wages paid to individuals from certain targeted groups), and the disabled access credit (applicable to expenditures by certain small businesses to make the businesses accessible to disabled individuals). Credits generally are determined based on a percentage of the cost associated with the underlying activity and generally are subject to certain limitations.

Affiliated group

Domestic corporations that are affiliated through 80 percent or more corporate ownership may elect to file a consolidated return in lieu of filing separate returns. For purposes of calculating tax liability, corporations filing a consolidated return generally are treated as

---

[30] For example, the carrying costs of tax-exempt State and local obligations and the premiums on certain life insurance policies are not deductible.

[31] At the fully phased-in nine percent deduction, a corporation is taxed at a rate of 35 percent on only 91 percent of qualifying income, resulting in an effective tax rate on qualifying income of 31.85 percent (0.91 x 0.35 = 0.3185). A similar reduction applies to the graduated rates applicable to individuals with qualifying domestic production activities income.

divisions of a single corporation; thus, the losses (and credits) of one corporation generally can offset the income (and thus reduce the otherwise applicable tax) of other affiliated corporations.

Alternative minimum tax

A corporation is subject to an alternative minimum tax which is payable, in addition to all other tax liabilities, to the extent that it exceeds the corporation's regular income tax liability. The tax is imposed at a flat rate of 20 percent on alternative minimum taxable income in excess of a $40,000 exemption amount.[32] Credits that are allowed to offset a corporation's regular tax liability generally are not allowed to offset its minimum tax liability. If a corporation pays the alternative minimum tax, the amount of the tax paid is allowed as a credit against the regular tax in future years.

Alternative minimum taxable income is the corporation's taxable income increased by the corporation's tax preference items and adjusted by determining the tax treatment of certain items in a manner that negates the deferral of income resulting from the regular tax treatment of those items. Among the preferences and adjustments applicable to the corporate alternative minimum tax are accelerated depreciation on certain property, certain expenses and allowances related to oil and gas and mining exploration and development, certain amortization expenses related to pollution control facilities, net operating losses and certain tax-exempt interest income. In addition, corporate alternative minimum taxable income is increased by 75 percent of the amount by which the corporation's "adjusted current earnings" exceeds its alternative minimum taxable income (determined without regard to this adjustment). Adjusted current earnings generally are determined with reference to the rules that apply in determining a corporation's earnings and profits.

Treatment of corporate distributions

The taxation of a corporation generally is separate and distinct from the taxation of its shareholders. A distribution by a corporation to one of its shareholders generally is taxable as a dividend to the shareholder to the extent of the corporation's current or accumulated earnings and profits, and such a distribution is not a deductible expense of the corporation.[33] Thus, the amount of a corporate dividend generally is taxed twice: once when the income is earned by the corporation and again when the dividend is distributed to the shareholder.[34]

---

[32] The exemption amount is phased out for corporations with income above certain thresholds, and is completely phased out for corporations with alternative minimum taxable income of $310,000 or more.

[33] A distribution in excess of the earnings and profits of a corporation generally is a tax-free return of capital to the shareholder to the extent of the shareholder's adjusted basis (generally, cost) in the stock of the corporation; such distribution is a capital gain if in excess of basis. A distribution of property other than cash generally is treated as a taxable sale of such property by the corporation and is taken into account by the shareholder at the property's fair market value. A distribution of common stock of the corporation generally is not a taxable event to either the corporation or the shareholder.

[34] This double taxation is mitigated by a reduced maximum tax rate of 15 percent generally applicable to dividend income of individuals (prior to 2011). Note that amounts paid as interest to the debtholders of a

Amounts received by a shareholder in complete liquidation of a corporation generally are treated as full payment in exchange for the shareholder's stock. A liquidating corporation recognizes gain or loss on the distributed property as if such property were sold to the distributee for its fair market value. However, if a corporation liquidates a subsidiary corporation of which it has 80 percent or more control, no gain or loss generally is recognized by either the parent corporation or the subsidiary corporation.

Accumulated earnings and personal holding company taxes

Taxes at the top rate generally applicable to dividend income of individuals (currently 15 percent, and scheduled to increase to 39.6 percent in 2011) may be imposed upon the accumulated earnings or personal holding company income of a corporation. The accumulated earnings tax may be imposed if a corporation retains earnings in excess of reasonable business needs. The personal holding company tax may be imposed on the excessive passive income of a closely held corporation. The accumulated earnings tax and the personal holding company tax are designed to ensure that both a corporate tax and a shareholder tax are effectively imposed on corporate earnings.

Tax treatment of foreign activities of U.S. corporations[35]

The United States employs a worldwide tax system, under which domestic corporations generally are taxed on all income, whether derived in the United States or abroad. Income earned by a domestic parent corporation from foreign operations conducted by foreign corporate subsidiaries generally is subject to U.S. tax when the income is distributed as a dividend to the domestic parent corporation. Until that repatriation, the U.S. tax on the income generally is deferred. However, certain anti-deferral regimes may cause the domestic parent corporation to be taxed on a current basis in the United States on certain categories of passive or highly mobile income earned by its foreign corporate subsidiaries, regardless of whether the income has been distributed as a dividend to the domestic parent corporation. The main anti-deferral regimes in this context are the controlled foreign corporation rules of subpart F[36] and the passive foreign investment company rules.[37] A foreign tax credit generally is available to offset, in whole or in part, the U.S. tax owed on foreign-source income, whether the income is earned directly by the domestic corporation, repatriated as an actual dividend, or included in the domestic parent corporation's income under one of the anti-deferral regimes.[38]

---

corporation generally are subject to only one level of tax (at the recipient level) because the corporation generally is allowed a deduction for the amount of interest expense paid or accrued.

[35] For more information regarding the tax treatment of the foreign activities of U.S. corporations, please see Joint Committee on Taxation, *The Impact of International Tax Reform: Background and Selected Issues Relating to U.S. International Tax Rules and the Competitiveness of U.S Businesses* (JCX-22-06), June 21, 2006.

[36] Secs. 951-964.

[37] Secs. 1291-1298.

[38] Secs. 901, 902, 960, 1291(g).

Corporate income tax rates since 1975

A corporation's regular income tax liability generally is determined by applying the appropriate tax rate to its taxable income. Table 3 below, provides a compilation of the marginal rates of tax imposed on corporate income from 1975 to 2010.

Table 3.–Federal Corporate Income Tax Rate Structure Since 1975[39]

Year	Corporate Taxable Income	Income Tax Rate (percent)
1975-78	First $25,000	20
	Next $25,000	22
	Over $50,000	48
1979-81	First $25,000	17
	$25,001-$50,000	20
	$50,001-$75,000	30
	$75,001-$100,000	40
	Over $100,000	46
1982	First $25,000	16
	$25,001-$50,000	19
	$50,001-$75,000	30
	$75,001-$100,000	40
	Over $100,000	46
1983	First $25,000	15
	$25,001-$50,000	18
	$50,001-$75,000	30
	$75,001-$100,000	40
	Over $100,000	46
1984-1986	First $25,000	15
	$25,001-$50,000	18
	$50,001-$75,000	30
	$75,001-$100,000	40
	$100,001-$1,000,000	46
	$1,000,001-$1,405,000	51*
	Over $1,405,000	46

---

[39] Internal Revenue Service. Corporation Income Tax Brackets and Rates, 1909-2002.

Year	Corporate Taxable Income	Income Tax Rate (percent)
1987[40]	First $25,000	15
	$25,001-$50,000	16.5
	$50,001-$75,000	27.5
	$75,001-$100,000	37
	$100,001-$335,000	42.5[*]
	$335,001-$1,000,000	40
	$1,000,001-$1,405,000	42.5[*]
	Over $1,405,000..	40
1988-1992	First $50,000	15
	$50,001-$75,000	25
	$75,001-$100,000	34
	$100,001-$335,000	39[*]
	Over $335,000...	34
1993-2010	First $50,000	15
	$50,001-$75,000	25
	$75,001-$100,000	34
	$100,001-$335,000	39[*]
	$335,001-$10,000,000	34
	$10,000,001-$15,000,000	35
	$15,000,001-$18,333,333	38[*]
	Over $18,333,333..	35

[*] Rates higher than the top bracket rate reflect phaseouts of the benefit from the lower bracket rates and are not technically the top corporate statutory rate.

---

[40] The Tax Reform Act of 1986 established a new rate structure effective for tax year 1988 and made the rates for transition year 1987 an average of the pre-1986 Tax Reform Act rates for 1986 and the post-1986 Tax Reform Act rates for 1988.

Figure 4, below, shows the top statutory corporate income tax rate and income threshold at which the rate begins to apply for selected years.

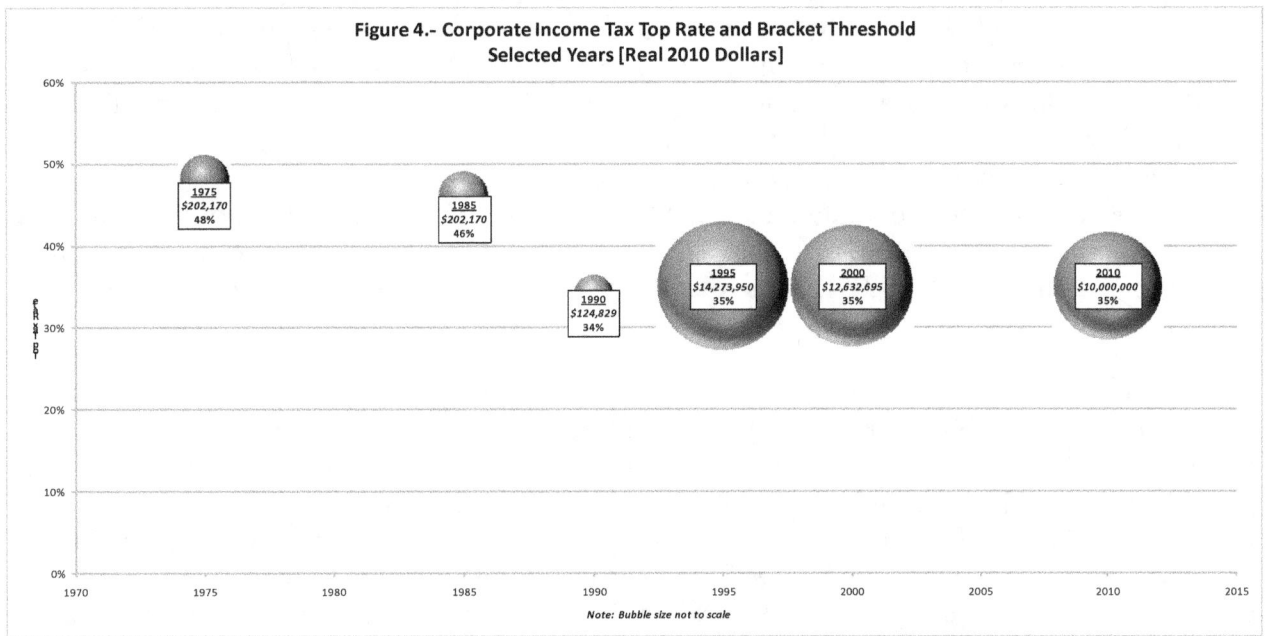

Figure 4.- Corporate Income Tax Top Rate and Bracket Threshold Selected Years [Real 2010 Dollars]

Significant modifications to the corporate income tax base since 1975[41]

The following discussion summarizes certain significant modifications to the corporate income tax base since 1975. In addition to affecting corporations, many of the Federal income tax provisions discussed below apply to all businesses.

Investment Tax Credit.—The Tax Rate Extension Act of 1962 created the investment tax credit.[42] The investment tax credit was originally seven percent (three percent in the case of certain public utilities) of investments in new tangible personal property and certain depreciable

---

[41] For additional discussion of U.S. Federal income tax provisions affecting businesses, see generally Joint Committee on Taxation, *Overview of the Federal Tax System as in Effect for 2008* (JCX-32-08), April 14, 2008; Joint Committee on Taxation, *Overview of Past Tax Legislation Providing Fiscal Stimulus and Issues in Designing and Delivering a Cash Rebate to Individuals*, (JCX-4-08), January 21, 2008; Joint Committee on Taxation, *Overview of the Federal Tax System as in Effect for 2007* (JCX-2-07), January 12, 2007; Joint Committee on Taxation, *Present Law and Background Relating to Selected Business Tax Issues* (JCX-41-06), September 19, 2006; Joint Committee on Taxation, *Background Materials on Business Tax Issues Prepared for the House Committee on Ways and Means Tax Policy Discussion Series* (JCX-23-02), April 4, 2002; Joint Committee on Taxation, Overview of Present Law and Selected Proposals Regarding the Federal Income Taxation of Small Business and Agriculture (JCX-45-02), May 31, 2002; Joint Committee on Taxation, *Study of the Overall State of the Federal Tax System and Recommendations for Simplification, Pursuant to Section 8022(3)(B) of the Internal Revenue Code of 1986* (JCS-3-01), April 2001; Joint Committee on Taxation, *Overview of Present Law and Selected Proposals Regarding the Federal Income Taxation of Small Business and Agriculture* (JCX-19-01), March 27, 2001. See also Jane G. Gravelle, *The Economic Effects of Taxing Capital Income* (1994); Joseph A. Pechman, *Federal Tax Policy* (5th ed.1987).

[42] Pub. L. No. 87-508, sec. 2 (1962).

real property (except buildings and structural components of buildings). No credit was allowed for property with a useful life of less than four years. For property with a life of four or five years, one-third of the investment was taken into account; for property with useful lives of six to eight years, two-thirds was taken into account; and for property with longer lives, the full amount of the investment was taken into account. Up to $50,000 of used property was eligible for the credit. The credit could offset tax liability in full up to $25,000, but above that amount, the credit could not reduce the tax liability by more than 25 percent. Any unused credit could be carried forward for five years and used in those years to the extent there was sufficient tax liability under the applicable limitation. If the property was sold before the end of its useful life, any excess credit was subject to recapture. The investment tax credit was suspended during the years 1966 and from 1969-1971. It was revived in 1972 and then increased to a rate of ten percent in 1975.

The Tax Reform Act of 1976 extended the 10 percent rate for the investment tax credit and continued the $100,000 limitation on qualified investment in used property from 1977 through 1980.[43] The Economic Recovery Tax Act of 1981 expanded eligible property to include petroleum storage facilities and certain rolling stock.[44] The used property limitation was increased to $125,000 for 1981 through 1984, and to $150,000 after 1984. A recapture provision was also added whereby the regular credit was recomputed upon early disposition by allowing a two-percent credit for each year the property was held (no recapture after five years, three years for eligible property). Additionally, the unused investment credits carry forward period increased from seven to 15 years, subject to certain limitations.

The Tax Reform Act of 1986 repealed the investment tax credit in an effort to equate effective tax rates with statutory tax rates and to rationalize the tax treatment of different assets.

Personal Service Corporations.–The Omnibus Budget Reconciliation Act of 1987 provided that, beginning in 1988, certain incorporated professional practices ("personal service corporations") are not eligible for graduated corporate rates but are taxed on all taxable income at the highest corporate income tax rate.[45]

Repeal of the *General Utilities* Doctrine.–In the Tax Reform Act of 1986, several corporate income tax provisions were modified to broaden the corporate income tax base and reduce the rates. Chief among these reforms was the repeal of the *General Utilities* doctrine. The Tax Reform Act of 1986 repealed a long-standing rule allowing an exception from the taxation of corporate earnings for unrealized or "built-in" gains held in corporate solution at the time of a liquidation of the corporation. This exception is generally viewed as originating in *General Utilities & Operating Company v. Helvering*,[46] and was later codified. The Tax Reform

---

[43] Pub. L. No. 94-555, secs. 801-2 (1976).

[44] Pub. L. No. 97-34, secs. 211 and 213 (1981).

[45] Pub. L. No. 100-203, sec. 10224 (1987).

[46] 196 U.S. 200 (1935).

Act of 1986 repealed the *General Utilities* doctrine, thereby generally requiring that a corporate-level tax be imposed on the built-in gains of a corporation upon its liquidation.[47] In the Omnibus Budget Reconciliation Act of 1987,[48] Congress clarified that the requirement of corporate-level taxation in cases of liquidations also extends to corporate dispositions utilizing subsidiaries—so-called mirror subsidiary transactions.

Taxation of Master Limited Partnerships ("MLPs").—An MLP is an investor-owned, publicly traded limited partnership that conducts business in a manner similar to a corporation. Prior to the Omnibus Budget Reconciliation Act of 1987, MLPs were taxable as partnerships and thereby exempt from corporate-level taxation. The 1987 Act required MLPs with active trade or business income (i.e., MLPs that do not derive most of their income from certain generally passive sources) to be treated as corporations for Federal tax purposes.

Corporate loss limitation following certain changes in stock ownership.—The Tax Reform Act of 1986 generally limited the amount of a corporation's pre-change losses that can be used annually following an ownership change to the tax-exempt rate multiplied by the value of the corporation at the time of the ownership change.[49] Prior law had imposed limits on corporate loss use following specified changes in ownership; generally with different results for stock purchases than for certain reorganizations.[50]

Depreciation.—Prior to 1981, the depreciation system was based on estimated useful lives determined either by using facts and circumstances or by using guideline lives in Treasury guidance.[51] The useful lives were generally applied to calculate depreciation deductions using a straight-line method. The Economic Recovery Tax Act of 1981 replaced the prior law depreciation system with the Accelerated Cost Recovery System ("ACRS") which significantly accelerated depreciation on tangible property.[52] ACRS is a system for recovering capital costs using accelerated methods over predetermined recovery periods that are generally unrelated to, but shorter than, prior law useful lives. For tangible personal property, the cost of eligible property was recovered over a 3, 5, 10, or 15-year period, depending on the type of property. The method used to calculate the depreciation expense was generally 150-percent declining balance (changing to straight-line) for property placed in service in 1981 through 1984, 175-percent declining balance (changing to straight line) for property placed in service in 1985, and 200-percent declining balance (changing to straight line) for property placed in service after

---

[47] The transactions subject to corporate level tax include the purchase of one corporation by another with an election to treat the transaction as an asset sale in which the buyer obtains a fair market value asset basis.

[48] Pub. L. No. 100-203, sec. 10223 (1987).

[49] Sec. 382 as amended by the Tax Reform Act of 1986, Pub. L. No. 99-514 (1986).

[50] See Joint Committee on Taxation, General Explanation of the Tax Reform Act of 1986, (JCS 10-87), pp. 288-294.

[51] See Rev. Proc. 62-21, 1962-2 C.B. 418, for guideline useful lives.

[52] Pub. L. No. 97-34, sec. 201 (1981).

1985. A half-year convention applied under which a taxpayer claimed a half-year of depreciation in the year tangible personal property was placed in service and no depreciation in the year in which such property was disposed. Under ACRS, the cost of real property was recovered over 15 years on either an accelerated or straight-line method and a mid-month convention. The Tax Equity and Fiscal Responsibility Act of 1982 ended the phase-in of faster depreciation methods and reduced the basis for depreciation by one-half the investment tax credit.[53]

The Tax Reform Act of 1986 created a new modified accelerated recovery system ("MACRS") that included six classes of tangible personal property (3, 5, 7, 10, 15 and 20 years), where the 3, 5, 7, and 10-year property classes are depreciated using 200 percent declining balance and the 15 and 20-year classes are depreciated using the 150 percent declining balance method. Real property is depreciated using the straight-line method, with residential rental property recovered over a 27.5 year period and nonresidential real property recovered over a 31.5-year period. In 1993, Congress increased the recovery period for nonresidential real property to 39 years.

The Job Creation and Worker Assistance Act of 2002[54] provided an additional first-year depreciation deduction equal to 30 percent of the adjusted basis of qualified property.[55] The additional first-year depreciation deduction was allowed for both regular tax and alternative minimum tax purposes for the taxable year in which the property was placed in service. The basis of the property and the depreciation allowances in the placed-in-service year and later years were appropriately adjusted to reflect the additional first-year depreciation deduction. In addition, there were no adjustments to the allowable amount of depreciation for purposes of computing a taxpayer's alternative minimum taxable income with respect to property to which the provision applies.

The Jobs and Growth Tax Relief Reconciliation Act of 2003[56] provided an additional first-year depreciation deduction equal to 50 percent of the adjusted basis of qualified property.[57] Qualified property was defined in the same manner as for purposes of the 30-percent additional first-year depreciation deduction, except that the applicable time period for acquisition or self construction of the property and placed in service date requirement were modified. Property for which the 50-percent additional first-year depreciation deduction was claimed was not eligible for the 30-percent additional first-year depreciation deduction. This provision also extended the placed in service date requirement for certain property with a recovery period of 10 years or

---

[53] Pub. L. No. 97-248 (1982).

[54] Pub. L. No. 107-147, sec. 101 (2002).

[55] A taxpayer was permitted to elect out of the 30-percent additional first-year depreciation deduction for any class of property for any taxable year.

[56] Pub. L. No. 108-27, sec. 201 (2003).

[57] A taxpayer was permitted to elect out of the 50-percent additional first-year depreciation deduction for any class of property for any taxable year.

longer and certain transportation property to property placed in service prior to January 1, 2006 (instead of January 1, 2005). Congress extended bonus depreciation in 2008, 2009 and 2010.[58]

Section 179 Expensing.–In lieu of depreciation, a taxpayer with a sufficiently small amount of annual investment may elect to deduct (or "expense") such costs under section 179. The rules of section 179 were originally enacted in 1958.[59] The 1958 legislation provided that a taxpayer could elect to deduct, as additional first-year depreciation, 20 percent of the cost of certain depreciable property. The cost of property eligible for this treatment was limited to $10,000, and consequently, the deduction was limited to $2,000 for the taxable year. Section 179 property was defined as depreciable property with a useful life of six years or more that was acquired by purchase after 1957 for use in a trade or business or for holding for the production of income.

In 1981, when the ACRS depreciation rules were adopted (generally providing accelerated methods and shorter recovery periods for depreciation), the section 179 rules were also revised to provide expensing of a greater amount of capital purchases.[60] The 1981 legislation provided that, for taxable years beginning in 1982 and 1983, a taxpayer could elect to deduct up to $5,000 of the cost of qualifying property placed in service in the taxable year. The dollar limitation was increased to $7,500 for taxable years beginning in 1984 and 1985, and increased to $10,000 for taxable years beginning in 1986 and thereafter.[61] Qualifying property was defined as property acquired by purchase for use in a trade or business (not including property held merely for the production of income). The provision was subsequently modified to provide that the dollar limitation on the deductible amount is reduced (but not below zero) by the amount by which the cost of section 179 property placed in service during the taxable year exceeds a dollar threshold (currently $400,000).[62]

The dollar limitation was further increased in 1993 to $17,500 for taxable years beginning after 1992.[63] In 1996, the expensing provisions were amended to provide for the

---

[58] The Economic Stimulus Act of 2008, Pub. L. No. 110-185 (2008), permitted taxpayers to take an additional first-year depreciation deduction equal to 50 percent of the adjusted basis of qualified property generally placed in service in 2008 (2009 for certain longer-lived or transportation property). The American Recovery and Reinvestment Act of 2009, Pub. L. No. 111-5 (2009), extended the additional first-year depreciation deduction for property placed in service in 2009 (2010 for certain longer-lived and transportation property). The Small Business Job Act of 2010, Pub. L. No. 111-240 (2010), extended the additional first year depreciation deduction for property placed in service in 2010 (2011 for certain longer-lived and transportation property).

[59] Pub. L. No. 85-866. sec. 204 (1958).

[60] Pub. L. No. 97-34, sec. 202 (1981).

[61] Subsequent legislation altered the years for which these amounts took effect. The $10,000 amount was to become effective for taxable years beginning in 1990 and thereafter, under section 13 of the Tax Reform Act of 1984, Pub. L. No. 98-369 (1984), but was made effective for taxable years beginning after 1986, under section 202 of the Tax Reform Act of 1986, Pub. L. No. 99-514 (1986).

[62] See sec. 202 of Pub. L. No. 99-514 (1986).

[63] Pub. L. No. 103-66, sec. 13116(a) (1993).

dollar limitation to increase over a period of several years, ultimately reaching $25,000 for taxable years beginning in 2003 or thereafter.[64] In 2003, the $25,000 limitation was increased to $100,000, and the phase-out level of $200,000 was increased to $400,000 for tax years beginning in 2002 through 2006.[65]

Prior to the enactment of the Small Business Jobs Act of 2010[66] and the Hiring Incentives to Restore Employment Act of 2010 (the "HIRE Act"),[67] section 179(b)(1) prescribed a $125,000 limitation on the aggregate cost of section 179 property that could be treated as an expense for taxable years beginning after 2006 and before 2011. For those same taxable years, section 179(b)(2) provided that the $125,000 amount is reduced by the amount by which the cost of section 179 property placed in service during the taxable years exceeds $500,000. Both the $125,000 amount and the $500,000 amount were adjusted for inflation annually under section 179(b)(5). The Economic Stimulus Act of 2008[68] changed the $125,000 amount and the $500,000 amount to $250,000 and $800,000, respectively, for taxable years beginning in 2008. The American Recovery and Reinvestment Tax Act of 2009[69] extended the $250,000 amount and the $800,000 amount to taxable years beginning in 2009. The HIRE Act changed the $125,000 amount and the $500,000 amount to $250,000 and $800,000, respectively, for taxable years beginning in 2010. Subsequently, the Small Business Jobs Act extended and increased the $250,000 amount and the $800,000 amount to $500,000 and $2,000,000, respectively, for taxable years beginning in 2010 and 2011.

Amortization of goodwill and certain other intangible assets.—The Omnibus Budget Reconciliation Act of 1993[70] specified a 15-year amortization period for acquired goodwill and certain other intangible assets. Under prior law, goodwill was not amortizable and the amortization of other intangible assets was generally based on facts and circumstances.

Net Operating Losses.—Prior to 1981, the Code generally allowed corporations incurring net operating losses ("NOLs") in one taxable year to carry back the loss as a deduction to the three prior taxable years and to carry forward the loss for seven years. In 1981, the NOL carry forward period was extended to 15 years for NOLs in taxable years ending after December 31, 1975.[71] The Taxpayer Relief Act of 1997 amended the Code to allow corporations to carry back

---

[64] Pub. L. No. 104-188, sec. 1111(a) (1996).

[65] Pub. L. No. 108-27, sec. 202 (2003).

[66] Pub. L. No. 111-240 (2010).

[67] Pub. L. No. 111-147 (2010).

[68] Pub. L. No. 110-185 (2008).

[69] Pub. L. No. 111-5 (2009).

[70] Pub. L. No. 103-66 (1993).

[71] Economic Recovery Tax Act of 1981, Pub. L. No. 97-34, sec. 207 (1981). NOLs of financial institutions were not modified; a carryback of 10 years and carryforward of five years was retained.

NOLs for two years and to carry NOLs forward for 20 years.[72] In 2002, the net operating loss carry back period was temporarily increased to five years for NOLs arising in taxable years ending in 2001 and 2002.[73] In addition, NOL carry backs arising in taxable years ending in 2001 and 2002, as well as NOL carry forwards to those taxable years, were allowed to offset 100 percent of a taxpayer's alternative minimum taxable income.[74]

The American Recovery and Reinvestment Act of 2009 provided eligible small business with an election to increase the carryback period for an applicable 2008 NOL from two years to any whole number of years elected by the taxpayer that is more than two and fewer than six.[75] An eligible small business is a taxpayer meeting a $15,000,000 gross receipts test. An applicable NOL is the taxpayer's NOL for any taxable year ending in 2008, or if elected by the taxpayer, the NOL for any taxable year beginning in 2008. The Worker, Homeownership, and Business Assistance Act of 2009 generally expanded the five-year NOL carryback election to any applicable NOLs arising in a taxable year beginning or ending in either 2008 or 2009.[76]

Add-on Minimum Tax.–From 1969 through 1986, corporations were subject to an "add-on minimum tax" on certain "tax preference" items (such as percentage depletion, accelerated depreciation, etc.) above a certain amount. For tax years 1969 through 1976, the tax was 10 percent of tax preferences in excess of $30,000; after 1976, the tax was 15 percent of preferences in excess of the greater of $10,000 or regular income tax.

Alternative Minimum Tax.–The alternative minimum tax ("AMT") replaced the add-on minimum tax, effective in 1987. It required a calculation of an alternative measure of taxable income that reduced or eliminated many tax preference items. The tax was 20 percent of the excess of this "alternative minimum taxable income" ("AMTI") over $40,000.[77] The $40,000 exemption was reduced by 25 percent of the excess of AMTI over $150,000. AMT in excess of regular tax could be carried over as a credit against regular tax in future years. Credits that are allowed to offset a corporation's regular tax liability generally are not allowed to offset its minimum tax liability. The Taxpayer Relief Act of 1997 repealed the AMT for small corporations (generally those with average gross receipts of less than $5 million).

---

[72] Pub. L. No. 105-34, sec. 1082 (1997).

[73] Job Creation and Worker Assistance Act of 2002, Pub. L. No. 107-147, sec. 102 (2002).

[74] Absent this special rule, NOL carryovers are only permitted to offset 90 percent of a taxpayer's alternative minimum taxable income. Sec. 56(d)(1)(A).

[75] Pub. L. No. 111-5 (2009).

[76] Pub. L. No. 111-92 (2009).

[77] The exemption amount is phased out for corporations with income above certain thresholds, and is completely phased out for corporations with alternative minimum taxable income of $310,000 or more.

High Yield Debt with Original Issue Discount.–In the Omnibus Budget Reconciliation Act of 1989,[78] Congress modified the tax treatment of instruments paying a rate of interest in excess of prevailing commercial rates that do not pay such interest on a current basis, such as certain original issue discount bonds. Under the 1989 Act, excessive yield rates in such cases are not deductible by the issuer. The nondeductible portion is treated as a dividend for purposes of the corporate dividends-received deduction.

Earnings Stripping.–An earnings stripping transaction is generally the payment of "excessive" deductible interest by a U.S. corporation to a related person when such interest is tax exempt (or partially tax exempt) in the hands of the related person. The Omnibus Budget Reconciliation Act of 1989 curbed the ability of foreign investors and other tax-exempt entities to use earning stripping transactions to obtain a competitive advantage over domestic corporate taxpayers.

---

[78] Pub. L. No. 101-239 (1989).

D. Estate and Gift Tax

The United States generally imposes a gift tax on transfers of property by gift made by a U.S. citizen or resident, whether made directly or indirectly and whether made in trust or otherwise. Nonresident aliens are subject to the gift tax with respect to transfers of tangible real or personal property where the property is located in the United States at the time of the gift. An estate tax generally is imposed on the taxable estate of any person who was a citizen or resident of the United States at the time of death and on certain property held by a nonresident alien if the property is located in the United States at the time of death. The estate tax is imposed on the estate of the decedent and generally is based on the fair market value of the property passing at death.[79] The taxable estate generally equals the worldwide gross estate less certain allowable deductions.

In 1975 the estate and gift tax systems were two separate systems. The gift tax laws provided for an annual exclusion of $3,000 per donee, plus a lifetime exemption of $30,000. Gift tax was computed using a graduated rate structure, with a maximum gift tax rate of 57.75 percent applicable to cumulative lifetime taxable transfers over $10 million. Property transferred by gift generally received a carry-over basis.

The estate tax exemption in 1975 was $60,000. Estate tax was computed using a graduated rate structure with a maximum taxable rate of 77 percent; this top rate applied to taxable transfers at death of over $10 million. A marital deduction permitted the estate of the deceased spouse to deduct 50 percent of the value of property transferred to the surviving spouse. This generally had the effect of allowing both spouses to be taxed on one-half of the property's value, which generally resulted in similar treatment in community property states and non-community property states.[80] Property transferred at death received a "stepped-up" basis, or a basis generally equal to the fair market value at the time of death.

Although there have been many changes to the estate and gift tax laws over the years since 1975, there were three significant acts that substantially modified the estate and gift tax regimes. The Tax Reform Act of 1976 (the "1976 Act"), The Economic Recovery Act of 1981 (the "1981 Act"), and Economic Growth and Tax Relief Reconciliation Act of 2001 ("EGTRRA") are discussed briefly below.

---

[79] In addition to interests in property owned by the decedent at the time of death, the Federal estate tax also generally is imposed on (1) proceeds of life insurance that was either payable to the decedent's estate or in which the decedent had an incident of ownership at death, (2) property over which the decedent had a general power of appointment at death, (3) annuities purchased by the decedent or his employer that were payable to the decedent before death, (4) property held by the decedent as a joint tenants, (5) property transferred by the decedent before death in which the decedent retained a life estate or over which the decedent had the power to designate who could possess or enjoy the property, (6) property revocably transferred by the decedent before death, and (7) certain transfers taking effect at the death of the decedent.

[80] Revenue Act of 1948, 62 Stat. 110.

The estate and gift tax system was substantially modified by the 1976 Act.[81] A single graduated rate table was created for both cumulative inter vivos gifts and taxable transfers at death, with the value of the taxable estate stacked on top of cumulative lifetime gifts to determine the marginal rate applied to the estate at death. In 1977, the top marginal rate was 70 percent; this top rate applied to cumulative inter vivos transfers and bequests of more than $5 million. The gift tax and estate tax exemption amounts also were combined into a single "unified credit" which was phased-in over time. In 1977 the unified credit effectively exempted $120,667 of inter vivos transfers and/or bequests from tax, and when fully phased-in in 1980 effectively exempted $161,563. The gift tax annual exclusion remained at $3,000.

The 1976 Act changed the basis rules such that property acquired from a decedent generally received a carry-over basis, rather than a step-up in basis to fair market value. The carry-over basis rules were retroactively repealed in 1980.

Another significant change in the 1976 Act was the introduction of an additional transfer tax on generation-skipping transfers. The generation-skipping transfer tax was designed to impose an additional tax on transfers which split enjoyment and ownership of property between two generations; generally where a beneficiary in the child's generation was given the right to use and benefit from property during life and a beneficiary in the grandchild's generation was given complete ownership of the property at the termination of the first interest.[82] The tax imposed was generally equal to the rates which would have applied if the property had been transferred outright by the donor and again by the first beneficiary.[83]

The Act also provided for a 100-percent marital deduction for the first $250,000 of property transferred to a surviving spouse.[84]

The Economic Recovery Act of 1981 (the "1981 Act")[85] made a number of additional changes to the estate and gift tax rules, many of which either had the effect of reducing the number of taxable estates or reducing or eliminating taxes on transfers between spouses. For example, the 1981 Act increased the unified credit such that, when fully phased in by 1987, the unified credit effectively exempted the first $600,000 of transfers from the unified estate and gift

---

[81] Pub. L. No. 94-455 (Oct. 4, 1976).

[82] Without the generation-skipping transfer tax, such a bequest had resulted in estate or gift taxation of the property to the donor and the second beneficiary, but not the intervening, first beneficiary. The generation-skipping transfer tax added a complex series of rules which generally treated the termination of the first beneficiary's interest as a taxable event.

[83] The generation-skipping transfer tax was substantially altered in the Tax Reform Act of 1986 by applying a single rate of tax equal to the highest marginal estate tax rate (55 percent at the time) to all generation-skipping transfers over $1 million. The Act also broadened the definition of generation-skipping transfer to include "direct skips" (e.g. direct transfers from a grandparent to a grandchild).

[84] The 1976 Act included other changes beyond the scope of this document.

[85] Pub. L. No. 97-35 (Aug. 13, 1981). The 1981 Act included other changes beyond the scope of this document.

tax, and gradually reduced the top marginal estate and gift tax rate from 70 percent to 50 percent over a four-year period (1982 through 1985).[86] The 1981 Act increased the annual gift tax exemption from $3,000 per donee to $10,000 per donee. Furthermore, the 1981 Act generally provided for unlimited deductions for gifts and bequests to spouses.[87]

The Taxpayer Relief Act of 1997[88] provided for gradual increase in the unified credit effective exemption amount from $625,000 in 1998 to $1 million in 2006 and thereafter.

EGTRRA gradually reduced and temporarily repealed the Federal estate and generation-skipping taxes. EGTRRA reduced the estate and generation-skipping taxes through 2009 by gradually increasing the estate tax exemption to $3.5 million and reducing the top estate tax rate to 45 percent. During that time, the gift tax exemption for lifetime transfers remained at $1 million; a common graduated rate table continued to apply for gift and estate tax purposes. In 2010, the estate and generation-skipping taxes are repealed, though only for one year. Modified carry-over basis rules apply to assets acquired from a decedent who dies in 2010. During 2010, the gift tax exemption remains at $1 million and taxable gifts are subject to a 35-percent rate.

The estate, gift, and generation-skipping transfer tax provisions of EGTRRA are scheduled to sunset after 2010, such that those provisions (including repeal of the estate and generation-skipping transfer taxes) do not apply to estates of decedents dying, gifts made, or generation-skipping transfers made after December 31, 2010. As a result, in general, the estate, gift, and generation-skipping transfer tax rates and exemption amounts that would have been in effect had EGTRRA not been enacted apply for estates of decedents dying, gifts made, or generation-skipping transfers made in 2011 and later years. A single graduated rate schedule with a top rate of 55 percent and a single effective exemption amount of $1 million applies for purposes of determining the tax on cumulative taxable transfers made by a taxpayer through lifetime gift or bequest.

---

[86] Subsequent legislation delayed the decrease in tax rates. The maximum estate and gift tax rates dropped to 50 percent after December 31, 1992, but the Omnibus Budget Reconciliation Act of 1993, Pub. L. No. 103-66 (August 10, 1993) restored the 55- percent top rate retroactively to January 1, 1993, and made that top rate permanent.

[87] Pub. L. No. 97-35 (Aug. 13, 1981).

[88] Pub. L. No. 105-34 (August 5, 1997).

Table 4.–Estate and Gift Tax Rates and Exemption Amounts, 1975-2010

Year	Annual gift exclusion	Exemption Value of Unified Credit (gift exemption when not unified)	Threshold of Highest Statutory Tax Rate	Highest Statutory Tax Rate (percent)
1975-1976	$3,000	$60,000 ($30,000)	$10 million	57.75 gift; 77 estate[1]
1977	$3,000	$120,667	$5 million	70
1978	$3,000	$134,000	$5 million	70
1979	$3,000	$147,333	$5 million	70
1980	$3,000	$161,563	$5 million	70
1981	$10,000	$175,625	$5 million	70
1982	$10,000	$225,000	$4 million	65
1983	$10,000	$275,000	$3.5 million	60
1984	$10,000	$325,000	$3 million	55
1985	$10,000	$400,000	$3 million	55
1986	$10,000	$500,000	$3 million	55
1987-1997	$10,000	$600,000	$3 million	55
1998	$10,000	$625,000	$3 million	55
1999	$10,000	$650,000	$3 million	55
2000-2001	$10,000	$675,000	$3 million	55
2002	$11,000	$1 million	$2.5 million	50
2003	$11,000	$1 million	$2 million	49
2004	$11,000	$1.5 million ($1 million)	$2 million	48
2005	$11,000	$1.5 million ($1 million)	$2 million	47
2006	$12,000	$2 million ($1 million)	$2 million	46
2007-2008	$12,000	$2 million ($1 million)	$1.5 million	45
2009	$13,000	$3.5 million ($1 million)	$1.5 million	45
2010	$13,000	No estate tax ($1 million)	$1.5 million	35 gift; No estate tax[3]
2011	$13,000	$1 million	$3 million	55

E. Excise Taxes

The Federal tax system imposes excise taxes on selected goods and services. In addition to excise taxes the primary purpose of which is revenue production, excise taxes also are imposed to promote adherence to other policies (e.g. penalty excise taxes). Generally, excise taxes are taxes imposed on a per unit or ad valorem (i.e., percentage of price) basis on the production, importation, or sale of a specific good or service. Among the goods and services subject to U.S. excise taxes are motor fuels, alcoholic beverages, tobacco products, firearms, air and ship transportation, certain environmentally hazardous activities and products, coal, telephone communications, certain wagers, and vehicles lacking in fuel efficiency.[89] The largest excise taxes in terms of revenue (for fiscal year 2008) are those for gasoline motor fuels ($25.1 billion), diesel motor fuel ($9.3 billion), domestic air ticket taxes ($8.2 billion) and domestic cigarettes ($6.6 billion).

Revenues from certain Federal excise taxes are dedicated to trust funds (e.g., the Highway Trust Fund) for designated expenditure programs and revenues from other excise taxes (e.g., alcoholic beverages) go to the General Fund for general purpose expenditures.

The following summarizes the key changes to the major excise taxes since 1975.

Alcohol

Taxes are imposed at different rates for distilled spirits, wines, and beer and are imposed on these products when produced or imported.

1. Distilled Spirits

In 1975 the excise tax rate on alcohol was the same as it had been since 1951 at $10.50 per proof gallon, a rate that had been set to raise revenue for the Korean War. Domestically bottled alcohols were taxed at the proof gallon[90] rate by multiplying the proof of the spirit by the tax rate. Thus a 100 proof spirit was taxed at $10.50 per gallon, while an 80 proof spirit was taxed at $8.40 per gallon (0.8 * 10.50). Alcohol that was bottled before being imported, however, was taxed using the wine gallon method such that all bottles were taxed at $10.50 per gallon regardless of proof.

The Trade Agreements Act of 1979[91] (the "1979 Act") repealed the wine gallon method of taxing bottled distilled spirit imports so that import bottles are now taxed at the proof gallon, the same as domestically bottled alcohol. The 1979 Act also ended the complicated system of joint control of distilleries, which required the presence of IRS agents in order for many actions

---

[89] See, Joint Committee on Taxation, *Study of the Overall State of the Federal Tax System and Recommendations for Simplification, Pursuant to Section 8022(3)(B)of the Internal Revenue Code of 1986,* (JCS-3-01), April 2001, pp. 478-516 for a detailed description of the various Federal excise taxes.

[90] A proof gallon is one liquid gallon of spirits that is 50% alcohol at 60 degrees Fahrenheit.

[91] Pub. L. No. 96-39.

to be performed to insure collection of taxes, and instead treated distilleries as bonded premises.[92]

By 1984 the excise tax, in constant dollars, had decreased by more than 70 percent since 1951. Congress increased the tax by $2.00 to $12.50 per proof gallon in the 1984 Tax Reform Act.

As part of the Omnibus Budget Reconciliation Act of 1990,[93] Congress raised the rate on distilled spirits by $1.00 to $13.50, the present rate.

2. Beer

In 1975 the excise tax rate on beer was $9.00 per barrel, the rate from 1951 when excise taxes were increased to raise revenue for the Korean War.

In 1977, a special tax rate for small brewers was created. The lower rate of $7.00 per barrel applies to brewers who brew fewer than two million barrels a year. The lower rate applies to the first 60,000 barrels removed during the calendar year while the normal rate applies to all barrels after the first 60,000.

The Revenue Reconciliation Act of 1990[94] doubled the rate, making the new rate $18.00 per barrel. The small producer exception was retained.

3. Wine

The tax rate on wine in 1975 was set at a variety of rates depending on type and proof of the wine and ranged from $0.17 per wine gallon for still wines to $3.40 per wine gallon on sparkling wines. Wines with over 24 percent alcohol were taxed the same as distilled spirits. These rates had been in effect since 1951.

The rates remained in effect until the Revenue Reconciliation Act of 1990[95] when the rates were raised by $0.90 per wine gallon for all wines, except sparkling wines which remained at $3.40 per wine gallon. The Act provided for a credit of up to $0.90 per wine gallon for small domestic producers (excluding sparkling wine) for the first 100,000 gallons of wine so that the tax remained roughly the same for those producers.

Until 1997 hard cider was taxed at the same rate as wine with alcohol less than 14 percent, or $1.07 per wine gallon. The tax rate for hard cider was decoupled from the wine rate

---

[92] In a bonded premises system the tax is determined and collected after bottling and when shipped. The changes also placed the burden of tax collection on the distilleries, rather than IRS agents, by requiring the distilleries to keep detailed and adequate records for inspection.

[93] Pub. L. No. 101-508.

[94] *Ibid.*

[95] *Ibid.*

and lowered to 22.6 cents per gallon under the Taxpayer Relief Act of 1997 (the "1997 Act"). The 1997 Act also significantly lowered the credit for small producers of hard cider, from the $0.90 cent credit per wine gallon applicable to wines to a $0.056 per gallon credit. Table 5 below, shows the alcohol excise tax rates.

Table 5.—Alcohol Excise Taxes

Type of Alcohol	1975	1985	1990-Present
Distilled Spirits (per proof gallon)	$10.50	$12.50	$13.50
Beer (per barrel)	9	9	18
Wines (per wine gallon)			
"Still wines" not more than 14 percent alcohol	.17	.17	1.07
"Still wines" 14-21% alcohol	.67	.67	1.57
"Still wines" 21-24% alcohol	2.25	2.25	3.15
"Still wines" more than 24% alcohol	Taxed as spirits	Taxed as Spirits	Taxed as Spirits
Champagne and sparkling wines	3.40	3.40	3.40
Artificially carbonated wines	2.40	2.40	3.30

Cigarettes

In 1975 the excise tax rate on small cigarettes was eight cents per pack, the same rate that had been in effect since 1951.[96] In Tax Equity and Fiscal Responsibility Act of 1982[97] the rate was doubled to 16 cents per pack, though the increase did not increase the per-pack tax in real terms over the level in 1951.[98] The next time the rates were raised was in the Revenue Reconciliation Act of 1990,[99] which increased the rate by eight cents per pack, half to take effect in 1991 and half to take effect in 1993.

---

[96] Small cigarettes are those weighing three pounds or less per thousand.

[97] Pub. L. No. 97-248.

[98] The tax rate in 1951 was eight cents per pack.

[99] Pub. L. No. 101-508.

The next tax increase came in the Balanced Budget Act of 1997[100] which again increased the rates in two stages. The first stage was a 10 cent increase in 2000, followed by an additional increase of five cents in 2002, leaving the rate at 39 cents per pack.

In 2009, the cigarette tax was raised roughly 156 percent to nearly $1.01 per pack as part of The Children's Health Insurance Program Reauthorization Act of 2009[101] in order to raise revenue. Table 6 below, shows the cigarette excise tax rates from 1975.

Table 6.–Cigarette Excise Tax Rates

Year	1975-1981	1982-1990	1991-1992	1993-1996	1997-2008	2009-Present
Small Cigarettes Tax Rate (cents per pack)	8	16[1]	20[2]	24[3]	39[4]	100.66[5]

Motor Fuels

4. Gasoline

The tax on gasoline in 1975 was 4 cents per gallon and the revenues raised from the tax were allocated to the Highway Trust Fund ("HTF"), created by the Highway Revenue Act of 1956.[102]

The gasoline tax was raised from 4 cents per gallon to nine cents per gallon in 1983 for the purpose of improving and repairing the nation's highways by the Surface Transportation Assistance Act of 1982.[103]

In 1986, the Resource Conservation and Recovery Act[104] created the Leaking Underground Storage Tank Trust Fund ("LUST"), which is funded by a 0.1 cent tax per gallon of

---

[100] Pub. L. No. 105-33.

[101] Pub. L. No. 111-3.

[102] Pub. L. No. 84-627.

[103] Pub. L. No. 97-424.

[104] Pub. L. No. 94-580.

gasoline. This raised the rate to 9.1 cents per gallon. The LUST tax has expired and been renewed multiple times since 1986.[105]

The next raise in the gasoline tax came in the Omnibus Budget Reconciliation Act of 1990 and was a measure taken in order to contribute to deficit reduction.[106] The gasoline tax at that time was increased to 14.1 cents per gallon, and the five cent increase was allocated half to the HTF and half to deficit reduction. The half allocated to the General Fund was a temporary allocation to end in 1995.

In 1993, the tax was increased to 18.4 cents per gallon by the Omnibus Budget Reconciliation Act of 1993.[107] The additional tax of 4.3 cents per gallon was earmarked to be used not for highway improvement but only for deficit reduction, and thus was allocated to the General Fund. The Taxpayer Relief Act of 1997 reallocated the 4.3 cent increase to the HTF.[108]

The current rate of 18.4 cents per gallon consists of 18.3 cents per gallon allocated to the HTF[109] and 0.1 cent per gallon allocated to the LUST fund.

5. Diesel

The tax on diesel fuel in 1975 was the same as the tax on gasoline,[110] and it too was raised from four cents to nine cents in 1983.[111] The tax was then increased again, without a corresponding increase in gasoline tax, in the Deficit Reduction Act of 1984.[112] At this time the tax was raised to 15 cents per gallon, in exchange for a reduction in the highway use tax on heavy trucks. The LUST tax in 1986 raised the tax to 15.1 cents per gallon.[113]

The diesel tax was raised by five cents in 1990 at the same time as the gasoline tax increase, similarly with half allocated to the General Fund and half allocated to the HTF.[114]

---

[105] The LUST tax expired from September 1990 until November 1990, January 1996 through September 1997, and April 2005 through September 2005. During those periods of time, the tax was .1 cent lower than indicated in the table.

[106] Pub. L. No. 101-508.

[107] Pub. L. No. 103-66.

[108] Pub. L. No. 105-34.

[109] 2.86 cents of this amount are allocated to the Mass Transit Account, a special account within the HTF.

[110] Pub. L. No. 84-627.

[111] Pub. L. No. 97-424

[112] Pub. L. No. 98-369.

[113] Pub. L. No. 94-580.

[114] Pub. L. No. 101-508.

The tax on diesel was again raised by the same amount as the gasoline tax, 4.3 cents, in 1993.[115]

As part of the Omnibus Budget Reconciliation Act of 1993, in order to prevent tax evasion schemes, the government moved the point of collection of the tax from the wholesale to the terminal level and mandated the dyeing of low-tax diesels.[116]

Farmers are exempt from paying the diesel excise tax when the diesel is used for farming purposes. Until 2005, farmers used a Certificate of Farming Use to buy clear (non-dyed) diesel without paying the tax. As part of the Safe, Accountable, Flexible and Efficient Transportation Equity Act[117] in 2005, farmers were required to pay the tax upfront and could later file a claim for a refund for the amounts used for farming purposes. Table 7 below, shows motor fuel excise tax rates from 1975.

Table 7.–Motor Fuel Excise Tax Rates

Year	1975	1983	1984	1987	1990	1993-Present
Gasoline (cents per gallon)	4	9	9	9.1	14.1	18.4
Diesel (cents per gallon)	4	9	15	15.1	20.1	24.4

---

[115] Pub. L. No. 103-66.

[116] Diesel used for off-road use such as construction and heating is generally not subject to tax and must be dyed red. State and local governments are exempt from the diesel tax even for highway use and generally must use diesel that is dyed blue.

[117] Pub. L. No. 109-59.

II. APPENDIX

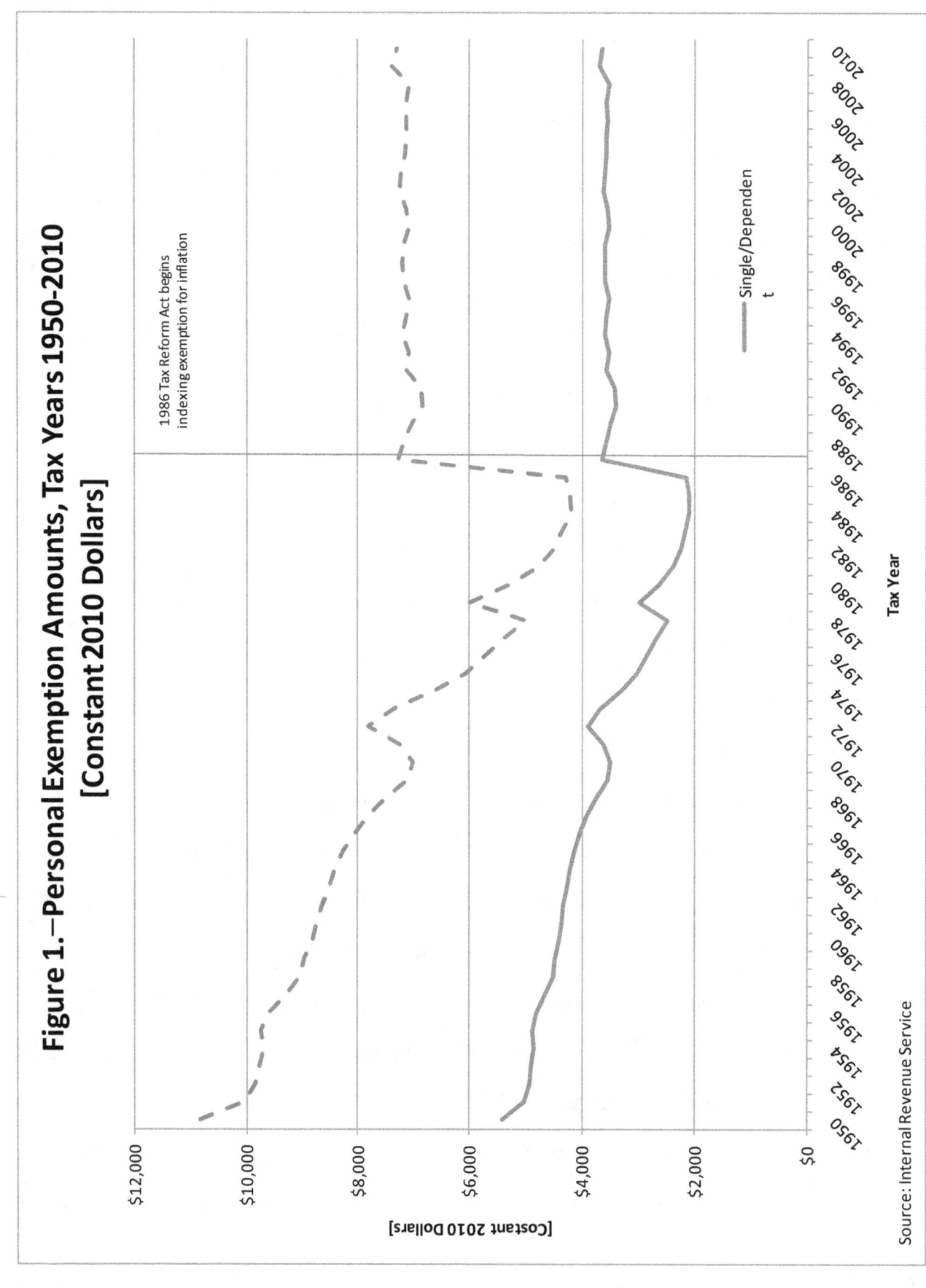

Figure 1.–Personal Exemption Amounts, Tax Years 1950-2010 [Constant 2010 Dollars]

1986 Tax Reform Act begins indexing exemption for inflation

—— Single/Dependent

Tax Year

[Constant 2010 Dollars]

Source: Internal Revenue Service

41

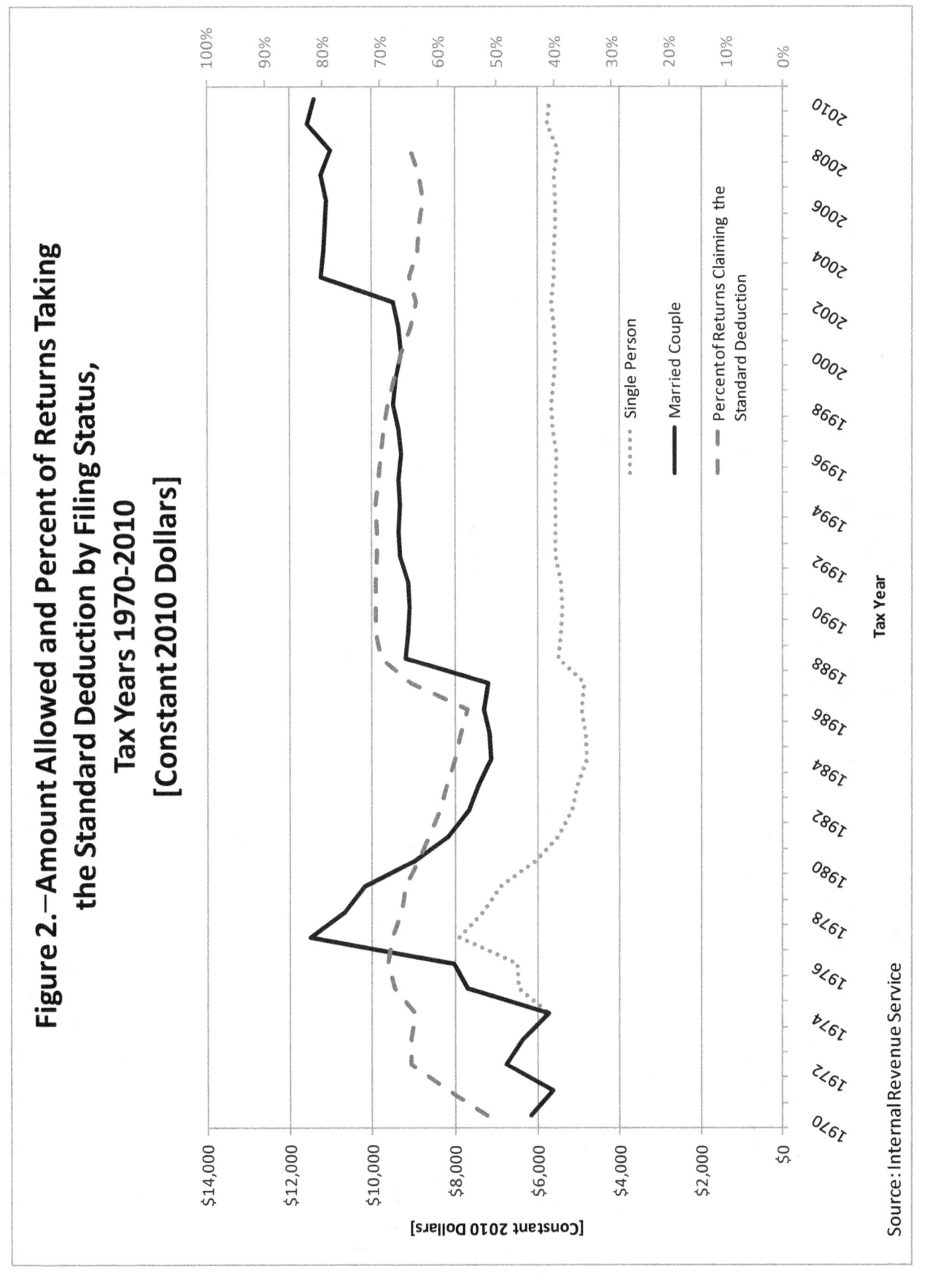

Figure 2.—Amount Allowed and Percent of Returns Taking the Standard Deduction by Filing Status, Tax Years 1970-2010 [Constant 2010 Dollars]

Source: Internal Revenue Service

42

Figure 3.–Individual Rate Bracket Structure
for Married Individuals Filing Joint Returns and Surviving Spouses
(Real 2010 Dollars)

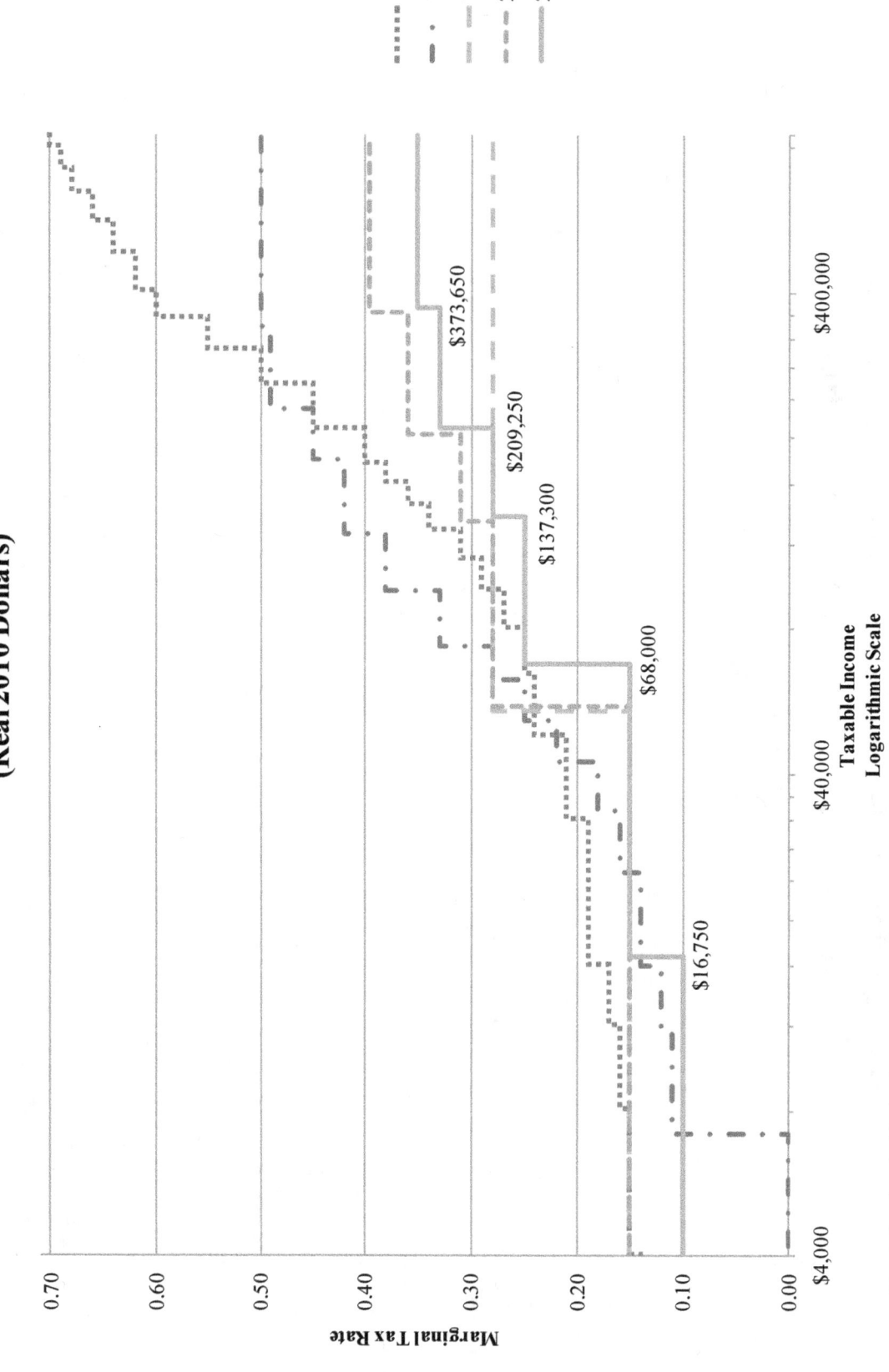

Note: The dollar thresholds for the rate brackets in 2010 are shown on the chart.

43

Year	Total Number of Returns	Number of Returns Claiming Standard Deduction	(% of Total)	Number of Returns Claiming Itemized Deduction	(% of Total)
		Table 1.–Number and Share of Returns Claiming Standard Deduction			
		Versus Itemized Deductions, Tax Years 1950-2008			
		[Millions of Returns]			
1950	53.1	42.7	80.4%	10.3	19.4%
1951	55.4	43.9	79.2%	11.6	20.9%
1952	56.5	43.7	77.3%	12.8	22.7%
1953	57.8	43.4	75.1%	14.4	24.9%
1954	56.7	41	72.3%	15.7	27.7%
1955	58.3	40.9	70.2%	16.9	29.0%
1956	59.2	40.3	68.1%	18.5	31.3%
1957	59.8	39.3	65.7%	20.2	33.8%
1958	59.1	37.9	64.1%	20.8	35.2%
1959	60.3	37.3	61.9%	22.5	37.3%
1960	61	36.5	59.8%	24.1	39.5%
1961	61.5	35.8	58.2%	25.3	41.1%
1962	62.7	35.8	57.1%	26.5	42.3%
1963	63.9	35.4	55.4%	28.2	44.1%
1964	65.4	38	58.1%	26.9	41.1%
1965	67.6	39.3	58.1%	27.9	41.3%
1966	70.2	41.2	58.7%	28.6	40.7%
1967	71.7	41.5	57.9%	29.8	41.6%
1968	73.7	41.3	56.0%	32	43.4%
1969	75.8	40.5	53.4%	34.9	46.0%
1970	74.3	38.4	51.7%	35.4	47.6%
1971	74.6	43.5	58.3%	30.7	41.2%
1972	77.6	50.2	64.7%	27	34.8%
1973	80.7	52.2	64.7%	28	34.7%
1974	83.3	53.2	63.9%	29.6	35.5%
1975	82.2	55.5	67.5%	26.1	31.8%
1976	84.7	58.2	68.7%	26	30.7%
1977	86.6	58.8	67.9%	22.9	26.4%
1978	89.8	59.5	66.3%	25.8	28.7%
1979	92.7	60.7	65.5%	26.5	28.6%
1980	93.9	59.5	63.4%	29	30.9%
1981	95.4	58.7	61.5%	31.6	33.1%
1982	95.3	56.9	59.7%	33.4	35.0%
1983	96.3	56.2	58.4%	35.2	36.6%
1984	99.4	56.7	57.0%	38.2	38.4%
1985	101.7	57	56.0%	39.8	39.1%
1986	103	56.5	54.9%	40.7	39.5%
1987	107	69.1	64.6%	35.6	33.3%
1988	109.7	76.5	69.7%	31.9	29.1%
1989	112.1	79.3	70.7%	32	28.5%

		Table 1.–Number and Share of Returns Claiming Standard Deduction Versus Itemized Deductions, Tax Years 1950-2008 (cont'd) [Millions of Returns]			
Year	Total Number of Returns	Number of Returns Claiming Standard Deduction	(% of Total)	Number of Returns Claiming Itemized Deduction	(% of Total)
1990	113.7	80.6	70.9%	32.2	28.3%
1991	114.7	81.3	70.9%	32.5	28.3%
1992	113.6	80.1	70.5%	32.5	28.6%
1993	114.6	80.8	70.5%	32.8	28.6%
1994	115.9	81.9	70.7%	33	28.5%
1995	118.2	83.2	70.4%	34	28.8%
1996	120.4	84	69.8%	35.4	29.4%
1997	122.4	84.8	69.3%	36.6	29.9%
1998	124.8	85.6	68.6%	38.2	30.6%
1999	127.1	85.8	67.5%	40.2	31.6%
2000	129.4	85.7	66.2%	42.5	32.8%
2001	130.3	84.2	64.6%	44.6	34.2%
2002	130.1	82.7	63.6%	45.6	35.0%
2003	130.4	84.6	64.9%	43.9	33.7%
2004	132.2	84	63.5%	46.3	35.0%
2005	134.4	84.8	63.1%	47.8	35.6%
2006	138.4	86.6	62.6%	49.1	35.5%
2007	143	90.5	63.3%	50.5	35.3%
2008 [p]	142.4	92	64.6%	48	33.7%

Source: Internal Revenue Service

[p] = preliminary

[3] Series revised, starting with the Spring 1997 SOI Bulletin, to exclude from the standard deduction statistics, the relatively small number of returns with no subject gross income and no deductions. Previously, these returns were classified as if they sshowed a standard deduction. For the 1977-1986 statistics, the standard deduction is the "zero bracket amount" (reported on returns with onoy a "zero bracket amount"). Such an amount was also included for a small number of returns for 1987-1988 for years in which the "zero bracket amount" was in effect, frequencies shown for standard deduction returns were derived by substracting the number reporting an income tax liability, but no itemized deductions, from the total of all returns. For 1950-1952, returns with no deductions and , for 1950-1954, the samll number with no income, regardless in these two categories were excluded from all the deduction statistics in this table.

Table 2.–Federal Individual Income Tax Rates for 1975

If taxable income is:	Then income tax equals:
Single Individuals	
Not over $500	14% of the taxable income
Over $500 but not over $1,000	$70 plus 15% of the excess over $500
Over $1,000 but not over $1,500	$145 plus 16% of the excess over $1,000
Over $1,500 but not over $2,000	$225 plus 17% of the excess over $1,500
Over $2,000 but not over $4,000	$310 plus 19% of the excess over $2,000
Over $4,000 but not over $6,000	$690 plus 21% of the excess over $4,000
Over $6,000 but not over $8,000	$1,110 plus 24% of the excess over $6,000
Over $8,000 but not over $10,000	$1,590 plus 25% of the excess over $8,000
Over $10,000 but not over $12,000	$2,090 plus 27% of the excess over $10,000
Over $12,000 but not over $14,000	$2,630 plus 29% of the excess over $12,000
Over $14,000 but not over $16,000	$3,210 plus 31% of the excess over $14,000
Over $16,000 but not over $18,000	$3,830 plus 34% of the excess over $16,000
Over $18,000 but not over $20,000	$4,510 plus 36% of the excess over $18,000
Over $20,000 but not over $22,000	$5,230 plus 38% of the excess over $20,000
Over $22,000 but not over $26,000	$5,990 plus 40% of the excess over $22,000
Over $26,000 but not over $32,000	$7,590 plus 45% of the excess over $26,000
Over $32,000 but not over $38,000	$10,290 plus 50% of the excess over $32,000
Over $38,000 but not over $44,000	$13,290 plus 55% of the excess over $38,000
Over $44,000 but not over $50,000	$16,590 plus 60% of the excess over $44,000
Over $50,000 but not over $60,000	$20,190 plus 62% of the excess over $50,000
Over $60,000 but not over $70,000	$26,390 plus 64% of the excess over $60,000
Over $70,000 but not over $80,000	$32,790 plus 66% of the excess over $70,000
Over $80,000 but not over $90,000	$39,390 plus 68% of the excess over $80,000
Over $90,000 but not over $100,000	$46,190 plus 69% of the excess over $90,000
Over $100,000	$53,090 plus 70% of the excess over $100,000

If taxable income is:	Then income tax equals:
Heads of Households	
Not over $1,000	14% of the taxable income
Over $1,000 but not over $2,000	$140 plus 16% of the excess over $1,000
Over $2,000 but not over $4,000	$300 plus 18% of the excess over $2,000
Over $4,000 but not over $6,000	$660 plus 19% of the excess over $4,000
Over $6,000 but not over $8,000	$1,040 plus 22% of the excess over $6,000
Over $8,000 but not over $10,000	$1,480 plus 23% of the excess over $8,000
Over $10,000 but not over $12,000	$1,940 plus 25% of the excess over $10,000
Over $12,000 but not over $14,000	$2,440 plus 27% of the excess over $12,000
Over $14,000 but not over $16,000	$2,980 plus 28% of the excess over $14,000
Over $16,000 but not over $18,000	$3,540 plus 31% of the excess over $16,000
Over $18,000 but not over $20,000	$4,160 plus 32% of the excess over $18,000
Over $20,000 but not over $22,000	$4,800 plus 35% of the excess over $20,000
Over $22,000 but not over $24,000	$5,500 plus 36% of the excess over $22,000
Over $24,000 but not over $26,000	$6,220 plus 38% of the excess over $24,000
Over $26,000 but not over $28,000	$6,980 plus 41% of the excess over $26,000
Over $28,000 but not over $32,000	$7,800 plus 42% of the excess over $28,000
Over $32,000 but not over $36,000	$9,480 plus 45% of the excess over $32,000
Over $36,000 but not over $38,000	$11,280 plus 48% of the excess over $36,000
Over $38,000 but not over $40,000	$12,240 plus 51% of the excess over $38,000
Over $40,000 but not over $44,000	$13,260 plus 52% of the excess over $40,000
Over $44,000 but not over $50,000	$15,340 plus 55% of the excess over $44,000
Over $50,000 but not over $52,000	$18,640 plus 56% of the excess over $50,000
Over $52,000 but not over $64,000	$19,760 plus 58% of the excess over $52,000
Over $64,000 but not over $70,000	$26,720 plus 59% of the excess over $64,000
Over $70,000 but not over $76,000	$30,260 plus 61% of the excess over $70,000
Over $76,000 but not over $80,000	$33,920 plus 62% of the excess over $76,000
Over $80,000 but not over $88,000	$36,400 plus 63% of the excess over $80,000
Over $88,000 but not over $100,000	$41,400 plus 64% of the excess over $88,000
Over $100,000 but not over $120,000	$49,120 plus 66% of the excess over $100,000
Over $120,000 but not over $140,000	$62,320 plus 67% of the excess over $120,000
Over $140,000 but not over $160,000	$75,720 plus 68% of the excess over $140,000

If taxable income is:	Then income tax equals:
Over $160,000 but not over $180,000	$89,320 plus 69% of the excess over $160,000
Over $180,000	$103,120 plus 70% of the excess over $180,000
Married Individuals Filing Joint Returns and Surviving Spouses	
Not over $1,000	14% of the taxable income
Over $1,000 but not over $2,000	$140 plus 15% of the excess over $1,000
Over $2,000 but not over $3,000	$290 plus 16% of the excess over $2,000
Over $3,000 but not over $4,000	$450 plus 17% of the excess over $3,000
Over $4,000 but not over $8,000	$620 plus 19% of the excess over $4,000
Over $8,000 but not over $12,000	$1,380 plus 22% of the excess over $8,000
Over $12,000 but not over $16,000	$2,260 plus 25% of the excess over $12,000
Over $16,000 but not over $20,000	$3,260 plus 28% of the excess over $16,000
Over $20,000 but not over $24,000	$4,380 plus 32% of the excess over $20,000
Over $24,000 but not over $28,000	$5,660 plus 36% of the excess over $24,000
Over $28,000 but not over $32,000	$7,100 plus 39% of the excess over $28,000
Over $32,000 but not over $36,000	$8,660 plus 42% of the excess over $32,000
Over $36,000 but not over $40,000	$10,340 plus 45% of the excess over $36,000
Over $40,000 but not over $44,000	$12,140 plus 48% of the excess over $40,000
Over $44,000 but not over $52,000	$14,060 plus 50% of the excess over $44,000
Over $52,000 but not over $64,000	$18,060 plus 53% of the excess over $52,000
Over $64,000 but not over $76,000	$24,420 plus 55% of the excess over $64,000
Over $76,000 but not over $88,000	$31,020 plus 58% of the excess over $76,000
Over $88,000 but not over $100,000	$37,980 plus 60% of the excess over $88,000
Over $100,000 but not over $120,000	$45,180 plus 62% of the excess over $100,000
Over $120,000 but not over $140,000	$57,580 plus 64% of the excess over $120,000
Over $140,000 but not over $160,000	$70,380 plus 66% of the excess over $140,000
Over $160,000 but not over $180,000	$83,580 plus 68% of the excess over $160,000
Over $180,000 but not over $200,000	$97,180 plus 69% of the excess over $180,000
Over $200,000	$110,980 plus 70% of the excess over $200,000

Married Individuals Filing Separate Returns	
Not over $500	14% of the taxable income
Over $500 but not over $1,000	$70 plus 15% of the excess over $500
Over $1,000 but not over $1,500	$145 plus 16% of the excess over $1,000
Over $1,500 but not over $2,000	$225 plus 17% of the excess over $1,500
Over $2,000 but not over $4,000	$310 plus 19% of the excess over $2,000
Over $4,000 but not over $6,000	$690 plus 22% of the excess over $4,000
Over $6,000 but not over $8,000	$1,130 plus 25% of the excess over $6,000
Over $8,000 but not over $10,000	$1,630 plus 28% of the excess over $8,000
Over $10,000 but not over $12,000	$2,190 plus 32% of the excess over $10,000
Over $12,000 but not over $14,000	$2,830 plus 36% of the excess over $12,000
Over $14,000 but not over $16,000	$3,550 plus 39% of the excess over $14,000
Over $16,000 but not over $18,000	$4,330 plus 42% of the excess over $16,000
Over $18,000 but not over $20,000	$5,170 plus 45% of the excess over $18,000
Over $20,000 but not over $22,000	$6,070 plus 48% of the excess over $20,000
Over $22,000 but not over $26,000	$7,030 plus 50% of the excess over $22,000
Over $26,000 but not over $32,000	$9,030 plus 53% of the excess over $26,000
Over $32,000 but not over $38,000	$12,210 plus 55% of the excess over $32,000
Over $38,000 but not over $44,000	$15,510 plus 58% of the excess over $38,000
Over $44,000 but not over $50,000	$18,990 plus 60% of the excess over $44,000
Over $50,000 but not over $60,000	$22,590 plus 62% of the excess over $50,000
Over $60,000 but not over $70,000	$28,790 plus 64% of the excess over $60,000
Over $70,000 but not over $80,000	$35,190 plus 66% of the excess over $70,000
Over $80,000 but not over $90,000	$41,790 plus 68% of the excess over $80,000
Over $90,000 but not over $100,000	$48,590 plus 69% of the excess over $90,000
Over $100,000	$55,490 plus 70% of the excess over $100,000

Table 3.–Federal Individual Income Tax Rates for 1985

If taxable income is:	Then income tax equals:
Single Individuals	
Not over $2,390	No tax
Over $2,390 but not over $3,540	11% of the excess over $2,390
Over $3,540 but not over $4,580	$126.50 plus 12% of the excess over $3,540
Over $4,580 but not over $6,760	$251.30 plus 14% of the excess over $4,580
Over $6,760 but not over $8,850	$556.50 plus 15% of the excess over $6,760
Over $8,850 but not over $11,240	$870 plus 16% of the excess over $8,850
Over $11,240 but not over $13,430	$1,252.40 plus 18% of the excess over $11,240
Over $13,430 but not over $15,610	$1,646.60 plus 20% of the excess over $13,430
Over $15,610 but not over $18,940	$2,082.60 plus 23% of the excess over $15,610
Over $18,940 but not over $24,460	$2,848.50 plus 26% of the excess over $18,940
Over $24,460 but not over $29,970	$4,283.70 plus 30% of the excess over $24,460
Over $29,970 but not over $35,490	$5,936.70 plus 34% of the excess over $29,970
Over $35,490 but not over $43,190	$7,813.50 plus 38% of the excess over $35,490
Over $43,190 but not over $57,550	$10,739.50 plus 42% of the excess over $43,190
Over $57,550 but not over $85,130	$16,770.70 plus 48% of the excess over $57,550
Over $85,130	$30,009.10 plus 50% of the excess over $85,130
Heads of Households	
Not over $2,390	No tax
Over $2,390 but not over $4,580	11% of the excess over $2,390
Over $4,580 but not over $6,760	$240.90 plus 12% of the excess over $4,580
Over $6,760 but not over $9,050	$502.50 plus 14% of the excess over $6,760
Over $9,050 but not over $12,280	$823.10 plus 17% of the excess over $8,850
Over $12,280 but not over $15,610	$1,372.20 plus 18% of the excess over $12,280
Over $15,610 but not over $18,940	$1,971.60 plus 20% of the excess over $15,610
Over $18,940 but not over $24,460	$2,637.60 plus 24% of the excess over $18,940
Over $24,460 but not over $29,970	$3,962.40 plus 28% of the excess over $24,460
Over $29,970 but not over $35,490	$5,505.20 plus 32% of the excess over $29,970
Over $35,490 but not over $46,520	$7,271.60 plus 35% of the excess over $35,490
Over $46,520 but not over $63,070	$11,132.10 plus 42% of the excess over $46,520

If taxable income is:	Then income tax equals:
Over $63,070 but not over $85,130	$18,083.10 plus 45% of the excess over $63,070
Over $85,130 but not over $112,720	$28,010.10 plus 48% of the excess over $85,130
Over $112,720	$41,253.30 plus 50% of the excess over $112,720

Married Individuals Filing Joint Returns and Surviving Spouses

If taxable income is:	Then income tax equals:
Not over $3,540	No tax
Over $3,540 but not over $5,720	11% of the excess over $3,540
Over $5,720 but not over $7,910	$239.80 plus 12% of the excess over $5,720
Over $7,910 but not over $12,390	$502.60 plus 14% of the excess over $7,910
Over $12,390 but not over $16,650	$1,129.80 plus 16% of the excess over $12,390
Over $16,650 but not over $21,020	$1,811.40 plus 18% of the excess over $16,650
Over $21,020 but not over $25,600	$2,598 plus 22% of the excess over $21,020
Over $25,600 but not over $31,120	$3,605.60 plus 25% of the excess over $25,600
Over $31,120 but not over $36,630	$4,985.60 plus 28% of the excess over $31,120
Over $36,630 but not over $47,670	$6,528.40 plus 33% of the excess over $36,630
Over $47,670 but not over $62,450	$10,171.60 plus 38% of the excess over $47,670
Over $62,450 but not over $89,090	$15,788 plus 42% of the excess over $62,450
Over $89,090 but not over $113,860	$26,976.80 plus 45% of the excess over $89,090
Over $113,860 but not over $169,020	$38,123.30 plus 49% of the excess over $113,860
Over $169,020	$65,151.70 plus 50% of the excess over $169,020

Married Individuals Filing Separate Returns

If taxable income is:	Then income tax equals:
Not over $1,770	No tax
Over $1,770 but not over $2,860	11% of the excess over $1,770
Over $2,860 but not over $3,955	$119.90 plus 12% of the excess over $2,860
Over $3,955 but not over $6,195	$251.30 plus 14% of the excess over $3,955
Over $6,195 but not over $8,325	$564.90 plus 16% of the excess over $6,195
Over $8,325 but not over $10,510	$905.70 plus 18% of the excess over $8,325
Over $10,510 but not over $12,800	$1,299 plus 22% of the excess over $10,510
Over $12,800 but not over $15,560	$1,802.80 plus 25% of the excess over $12,800
Over $15,560 but not over $18,315	$2,492.80 plus 28% of the excess over $15,560
Over $18,315 but not over $23,835	$3,264.20 plus 33% of the excess over $18,315
Over $23,835 but not over $31,225	$5,085.80 plus 38% of the excess over $23,835

If taxable income is:	Then income tax equals:
Over $31,225 but not over $44,545	$7,894 plus 42% of the excess over $31,225
Over $44,545 but not over $56,930	$13,488.40 plus 45% of the excess over $44,545
Over $56,930 but not over $84,510	$19,061.65 plus 49% of the excess over $56,930
Over $84,510	$32,575.85 plus 50% of the excess over $84,510

Table 4.–Federal Individual Income Tax Rates for 1990

If taxable income is:	Then income tax equals:
Single Individuals	
Not over $19,450	15% of the taxable income
Over $19,450	$2,917.50 plus 28% of the excess over $19,450[1]
Heads of Households	
Not over $26,050	15% of the taxable income
Over $26,050	$3,907.50 plus 28% of the excess over $26,050[1]
Married Individuals Filing Joint Returns and Surviving Spouses	
Not over $32,450	15% of the taxable income
Over $32,450	$4,867.50 plus 28% of the excess over $32,450[1]
Married Individuals Filing Separate Returns	
Not over $16,225	15% of the taxable income
Over $16,225	$2,433.75 plus 28% of the excess over $16,225[1]

[1] For taxable incomes above certain thresholds the combined benefit of the 15-percent rate bracket and any applicable personal exemptions of the taxpayer are recaptured through a five percentage point increase in the income tax rate resulting in an marginal tax rate of 33 percent. After the combined benefit of the 15-percent rate bracket and any applicable personal exemptions is recaptured the marginal rate again becomes 28 percent.

Table 5.–Federal Individual Income Tax Rates for 1995

If taxable income is:	Then income tax equals:
Single Individuals	
Not over $23,350	15% of the taxable income
Over $23,350 but not over $56,550	$3,502.50 plus 28% of the excess over $23,350
Over $56,550 but not over $117,950	$12,798.50 plus 31% of the excess over $56,550
Over $117,950 but not over $256,500	$31,832.50 plus 36% of the excess over $117,950
Over $256,500	$81,710.50 plus 39.6% of the excess over $256,500
Heads of Households	
Not over $31,250	15% of the taxable income
Over $31,250 but not over $80,750	$4,687.50 plus 28% of the excess over $31,250
Over $80,750 but not over $130,800	$18,547.50 plus 31% of the excess over $80,750
Over $130,800 but not over $256,500	$34,063 plus 36% of the excess over $130,800
Over $256,500	$79,315 plus 39.6% of the excess over $256,500
Married Individuals Filing Joint Returns and Surviving Spouses	
Not over $39,000	15% of the taxable income
Over $39,000 but not over $94,250	$5,850 plus 28% of the excess over $39,000
Over $94,250 but not over $143,600	$21,320 plus 31% of the excess over $94,250
Over $143,600 but not over $256,500	$36,618.50 plus 36% of the excess over $143,600
Over $256,500	$77,262.50 plus 39.6% of the excess over $256,500
Married Individuals Filing Separate Returns	
Not over $19,500	15% of the taxable income
Over $19,500 but not over $47,125	$2,925 plus 28% of the excess over $19,500
Over $47,125 but not over $71,800	$10,660 plus 31% of the excess over $47,125
Over $71,800 but not over $128,250	$18,309.25 plus 36% of the excess over $71,800
Over $128,250	$38,631.25 plus 39.6% of the excess over $128,250

Table 6.–Federal Individual Income Tax Rates for 2000

If taxable income is:	Then income tax equals:
Single Individuals	
Not over $26,250	15% of the taxable income
Over $26,250 but not over $63,550	$3,937.50 plus 28% of the excess over $26,250
Over $63,550 but not over $132,600	$14,381.50 plus 31% of the excess over $63,550
Over $132,600 but not over $288,350	$35,787 plus 36% of the excess over $132,600
Over $288,350	$91,857 plus 39.6% of the excess over $288,350
Heads of Households	
Not over $35,150	15% of the taxable income
Over $35,150 but not over $90,800	$5,272.50 plus 28% of the excess over $35,150
Over $90,800 but not over $140,050	$20,854.50 plus 31% of the excess over $90,800
Over $140,050 but not over $288,350	$38,292 plus 36% of the excess over $140,050
Over $288,350	$89,160 plus 39.6% of the excess over $288,350
Married Individuals Filing Joint Returns and Surviving Spouses	
Not over $43,850	15% of the taxable income
Over $43,850 but not over $105,950	$6,577.50 plus 28% of the excess over $43,850
Over $105,950 but not over $161,450	$23,965.50 plus 31% of the excess over $105,950
Over $161,450 but not over $288,350	$41,170.50 plus 36% of the excess over $161,450
Over $288,350	$86,854.50 plus 39.6% of the excess over $288,350
Married Individuals Filing Separate Returns	
Not over $21,965	15% of the taxable income
Over $21,965 but not over $52,975	$3,288.75 plus 28% of the excess over $21,965
Over $52,975 but not over $80,725	$11,982.75 plus 31% of the excess over $52,975
Over $80,725 but not over $144,175	$20,584.50 plus 36% of the excess over $80,725
Over $144,175	$43,427.25 plus 39.6% of the excess over $144,175

Table 7.–Federal Individual Income Tax Rates for 2010

If taxable income is:	Then income tax equals:
Single Individuals	
Not over $8,375	10% of the taxable income
Over $8,375 but not over $34,000	$837.50 plus 15% of the excess over $8,375
Over $34,000 but not over $82,400	$4,681.25 plus 25% of the excess over $34,000
Over $82,400 but not over $171,850	$16,781.25 plus 28% of the excess over $82,400
Over $171,850 but not over $373,650	$41,827.25 plus 33% of the excess over $171,850
Over $373,650	$108,421.25 plus 35% of the excess over $373,650
Heads of Households	
Not over $11,950	10% of the taxable income
Over $11,950 but not over $45,550	$1,195 plus 15% of the excess over $11,950
Over $45,550 but not over $117,650	$6,235 plus 25% of the excess over $45,550
Over $117,650 but not over $190,550	$24,260 plus 28% of the excess over $117,650
Over $190,550 but not over $373,650	$44,672 plus 33% of the excess over $190,550
Over $373,650	$105,095 plus 35% of the excess over $373,650
Married Individuals Filing Joint Returns and Surviving Spouses	
Not over $16,750	10% of the taxable income
Over $16,750 but not over $68,000	$1,675 plus 15% of the excess over $16,750
Over $68,000 but not over $137,300	$9,362.50 plus 25% of the excess over $68,000
Over $137,300 but not over $209,250	$26,687.50 plus 28% of the excess over $137,300
Over $209,250 but not over $373,650	$46,833.50 plus 33% of the excess over $209,250
Over $373,650	$101,085.50 plus 35% of the excess over $373,650
Married Individuals Filing Separate Returns	
Not over $8,375	10% of the taxable income
Over $8,375 but not over $34,000	$837.50 plus 15% of the excess over $8,375
Over $34,000 but not over $68,650	$4,681.25 plus 25% of the excess over $34,000
Over $68,650 but not over $104,625	$13,343.75 plus 28% of the excess over $68,650
Over $104,625 but not over $186,825	$23,416.75 plus 33% of the excess over $104,625
Over $186,825	$50,542.75 plus 35% of the excess over $186,825

Table 8.–Tax Treatment of Long-Term Capital Gains of Individuals, 1913-2010

Year	Holding Period	Percentage of long-term capital gains includible in income	Alternative tax rate on long-term capital gains, if any, or maximum marginal regular tax rate on long-term capital gains
1913-21	n/a	n/a	n/a (highest rate on ordinary income ranged from 7% to 77%)
1922-33	2 years or less	n/a	n/a (highest rate on ordinary income ranged from 24% to 73%)
	Over 2 years	50	12.5%
1934-37	1 year or less	n/a	n/a (highest rate on ordinary income ranged from 63% to 79%)
	Over 1 year to 2 years	80	50.4% in 1934-35; 63.2% in 1936-37
	Over 2 years to 5 years	60	50.4% in 1934-35; 63.2% in 1936-37
	Over 5 years to 10 years	40	25.2% in 1934-35; 31.6% in 1936-37
	Over 10 years	30	25.2% in 1934-35; 31.6% in 1936-37
1938-41	18 months or less	n/a	n/a (highest rate on ordinary income ranged from 79% to 81.1%)
	Over 18 months to 2 years	66.87	30% of included gain, which was equivalent to a 20% rate
	Over 2 years	50	30% of included gain, which was equivalent to a 15% rate

57

Year	Holding Period	Percentage of long-term capital gains includible in income	Alternative tax rate on long-term capital gains, if any, or maximum marginal regular tax rate on long-term capital gains
1942-67	6 months or less	n/a	n/a (highest rate on ordinary income ranged from 70% to 94%)
	Over 6 months	50	25% (26% in 1952-53)
1968-71	6 months or less	n/a	n/a (highest rate on ordinary income ranged from 70% to 77%)
	Over 6 months	50	35%
1972-76	6 months or less	n/a	n/a (highest rate on ordinary income: 70%)
	Over 6 months	50	35%
1977	9 months or less	n/a	n/a (highest rate on ordinary income: 70%)
	Over 9 months	50	35%
1978	1 year or less	n/a	n/a (highest rate on ordinary income: 70%)
	Over 1 year	50 for gains realized before 11/1/78; 40 after 10/31/78	35% for gains realized before 11/1/78; 28% after 10/31/78
1979-80	1 year or less	n/a	n/a (highest rate on ordinary income: 70%)
	Over 1 year	40	28%
1981	1 year or less	n/a	n/a (highest rate on ordinary income: 69.125%)

Year	Holding Period	Percentage of long-term capital gains includible in income	Alternative tax rate on long-term capital gains, if any, or maximum marginal regular tax rate on long-term capital gains
	Over 1 year	40	28% for gains realized before 6/10/81; 20% after 6/9/81
1982-86	1 year or less (6 months or less for assets acquired after 6/22/84 and before 1/1/88)	n/a	n/a (highest rate on ordinary income: 50%)
	Over 1 year (over 6 months for assets acquired after 6/22/84 and before 1/1/88)	40	20%
1987-90	1 year or less (6 months or less for assets acquired after 6/22/84 and before 1/1/88)	n/a	n/a (highest rate on ordinary income: 38/5% in 1987; 33% thereafter (28% for individuals in the highest income group))
	Over 1 year (over 6 months for assets acquired after 6/22/84 and before 1/1/88)	100	28% in 1987; 33% thereafter (28% for individuals in the highest income group)
1991-92	1 year or less	100	n/a (highest rate on ordinary income: 31%)
	Over 1 year	n/a	28%
1993-97	1 year or less	100	n/a (highest rate on ordinary income: 39/6%)
	Over 1 year	n/a	28%
1997-1998	1 year or less	100	n/a (highest rate on ordinary income: 39.6%)
	Over 1 year	n/a	20% for gains realized after 5/7/97, 10%

Year	Holding Period	Percentage of long-term capital gains includible in income	Alternative tax rate on long-term capital gains, if any, or maximum marginal regular tax rate on long-term capital gains
			for gain income that would otherwise be taxed in the 15%-bracket. Maximum rate remains 28% for collectibles. Recapture on sec. 1250 depreciation at 25%. A 50% exclusion for gains on sale of certain small business stock realized after 8/13/98 yields a maximum rate on qualifying stock at 14%.
1999-2000	1 year or less	100	n/a (highest rate on ordinary income: 39.6%)
	Over 1 year	n/a	20% (10% for gain income that would otherwise be taxed in the 15%-bracket). Maximum rate at 28% for collectibles. Recapture on sec. 1250 depreciation at 25%. Maximum rate on certain small business stock at 14%.
2001	1 year or less	100	n/a (highest rate on ordinary income: 39.1%)
	Over 1 year	n/a	20% (10% for gain income that would otherwise be taxed in the 15%-bracket). Maximum rate at 28% for collectibles. Recapture on sec. 1250 depreciation at 25%. Maximum rate on certain small business stock at 14%.

Year	Holding Period	Percentage of long-term capital gains includible in income	Alternative tax rate on long-term capital gains, if any, or maximum marginal regular tax rate on long-term capital gains
	Over 5 years	n/a	8% for gain on assets held for 5 or more years which otherwise would be taxed at 10% rate.
2002	1 year or less	100	n/a (highest rate on ordinary income: 38.6%)
	Over 1 year	n/a	20% (10% for gain income that would otherwise be taxed in the 15%-bracket). Maximum rate at 28% for collectibles. Recapture on sec. 1250 depreciation at 25%. Maximum rate on certain small business stock at 14%.
	Over 5 years	n/a	8% for gain on assets held for 5 or more years which otherwise would be taxed at 10 percent rate.
2003-2007	1 year or less	100	n/a (highest rate on ordinary income: 35%)
	Over 1 year	n/a	15% (5% for gain income that would otherwise be taxed in the 15%-bracket). Maximum rate at 28% for collectibles. Recapture on sec. 1250 depreciation at 25%. Maximum rate on certain small business stock at 14%.
2008-2010	1 year or less	100	n/a (highest rate on ordinary income: 35%)
	Over 1 year	n/a	15% (0% for gain income that would

61

Year	Holding Period	Percentage of long-term capital gains includible in income	Alternative tax rate on long-term capital gains, if any, or maximum marginal regular tax rate on long-term capital gains
			otherwise be taxed in the 15%-bracket). Maximum rate at 28% for collectibles. Recapture on sec. 1250 depreciation at 25%. Maximum rate on certain small business stock at 14%.

Table 9.–Earned Income Credit: Number of Recipients and Amount of Credit, 1975-2008

Year	Number of receipient families (thousands)	Total amount of credit ($ millions)	Refunded portion of credit ($ millions)	Average credit per family
1975	6,215	1,250	900	201
1976	6,473	1,295	890	200
1977	5,627	1,227	880	200
1978	5,192	1,048	801	202
1979	7,135	2,052	1,395	288
1980	6,954	1,986	1,370	286
1981	6,717	1,912	1,278	285
1982	6,395	1,775	1,222	278
1983	7,368	1,795	1,289	224
1984	6,376	1,638	1,162	257
1985	7,432	2,088	1,499	281
1986	7,156	2,009	1,479	281
1987	8,738	3,391	2,930	450
1988	11,148	5,896	4,257	529
1989	11,696	6,595	4,636	564
1990	12,542	7,542	5,266	601
1991	13,665	11,105	8,183	813
1992	14,097	13,028	9,959	924
1993	15,117	15,537	12,028	1,028
1994	19,017	21,105	16,598	1,110
1995	19,334	25,956	20,829	1,342
1996	19,464	28,825	23,157	1,481
1997	19,391	30,389	24,396	1,567
1998	20,273	32,340	27,175	1,595
1999	19,259	31,901	27,604	1,656
2000	19,277	32,296	27,803	1,675
2001	19,593	33,376	29,043	1,704
2002	21,703	38,199	33,737	1,760
2003	22,024	38,657	24,012	1,755
2004	22,270	40,024	35,300	1,797
2005	22,752	42,410	37,465	1,864
2006	23,042	44,388	39,072	1,926
2007	24,584	48,540	42,508	1,974
2008	24,757	50,669	44,260	2,047

Source: Internal Revenue Service.

Figure 4.–Number of Returns by Filing Status, Percent of Total

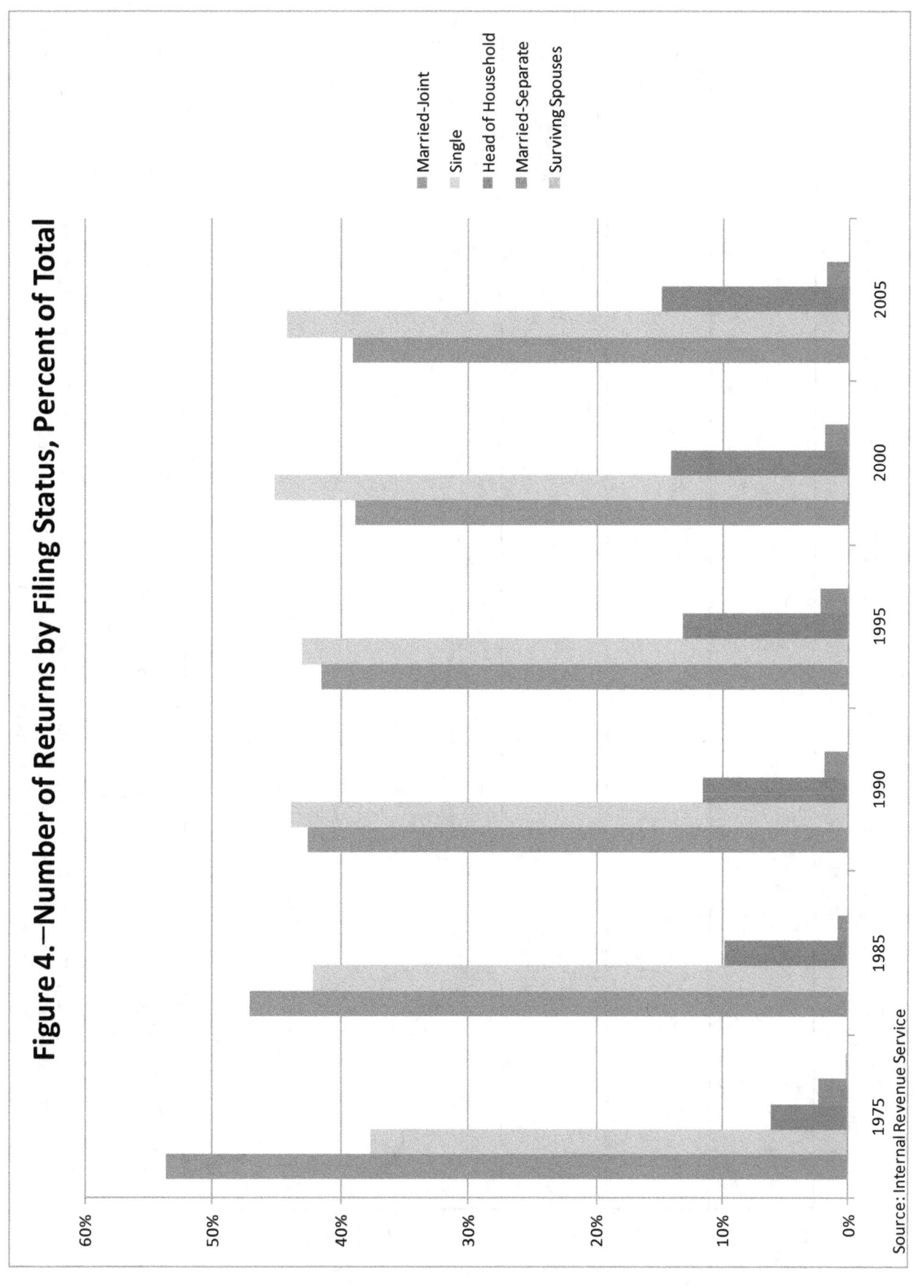

Married-Joint
Single
Head of Household
Married-Separate
Surviving Spouses

Source: Internal Revenue Service

64

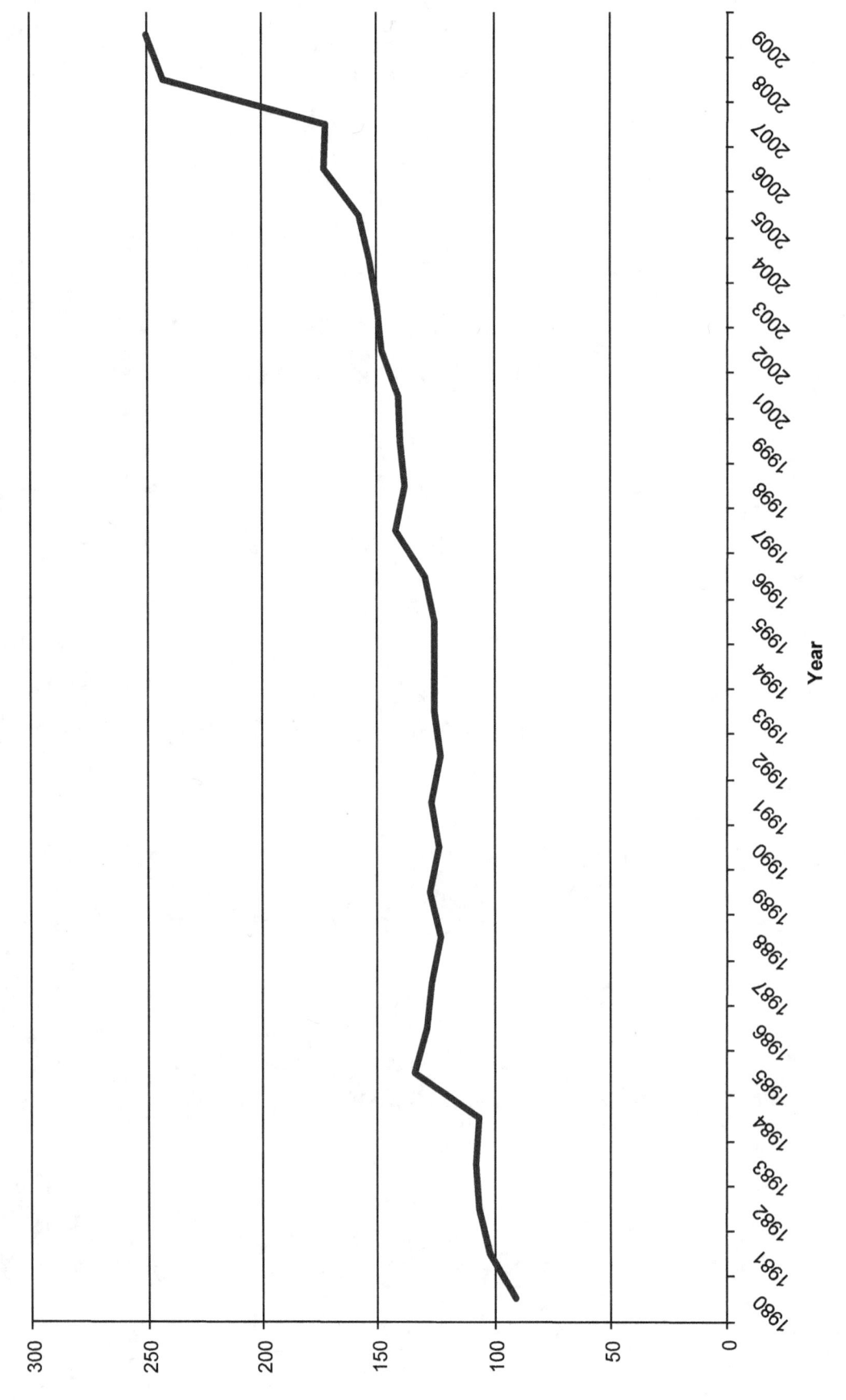

Figure 5.–Joint Committee on Taxation Count of Tax Expenditures, 1980-2009

Year

Note: This chart shows the number of tax expenditures listed in the tables that appear in the Joint Committee on Taxation's annual pamphlet on tax expenditures. Certain methodological changes in how tax expenditures were defined and listed, notably expanded breakouts of certain tax provisions formerly listed as a single tax expenditure, account for the bulk of the substantial rise in listed tax expenditures from 2007 to 2008.

Table 10.–Aggregate Federal Receipts by Source, 1950-2009
[millions of dollars]

Fiscal Year	Individual Income Tax	Corporate Income Tax	Employment[1] Taxes	Excise Taxes	Estate and Gift Taxes	Other[2] Receipts	Total
1950	15,755	10,449	4,338	7,550	698	653	39,443
1951	21,616	14,101	5,674	8,648	708	870	51,616
1952	27,934	21,226	6,445	8,852	818	892	66,167
1953	29,816	21,238	6,820	9,877	881	976	69,608
1954	29,542	21,101	7,208	9,945	934	971	69,701
1955	28,747	17,861	7,862	9,131	924	926	65,451
1956	32,188	20,880	9,320	9,929	1,161	1,109	74,587
1957	35,620	21,167	9,997	10,534	1,365	1,307	79,990
1958	34,724	20,074	11,239	10,638	1,393	1,568	79,636
1959	36,719	17,309	11,722	10,578	1,333	1,588	79,249
1960	40,715	21,494	14,683	11,676	1,606	2,317	92,492
1961	41,338	20,954	16,439	11,860	1,896	1,900	94,388
1962	45,571	20,523	17,046	12,534	2,016	1,985	99,676
1963	47,588	21,579	19,804	13,194	2,167	2,228	106,560
1964	48,697	23,493	21,963	13,731	2,394	2,337	112,613
1965	48,792	25,461	22,242	14,570	2,716	3,037	116,817
1966	55,446	30,073	25,546	13,062	3,066	3,642	130,835
1967	61,526	33,971	32,619	13,719	2,978	4,009	148,822
1968	68,726	28,665	33,923	14,079	3,051	4,529	152,973
1969	87,249	36,678	39,015	15,222	3,491	5,227	186,882
1970	90,412	32,829	44,362	15,705	3,644	5,855	192,807
1971	86,230	26,785	47,325	16,614	3,735	6,450	187,139
1972	94,737	32,166	52,574	15,477	5,436	6,919	207,309
1973	103,246	36,153	63,115	16,260	4,917	7,109	230,799
1974	118,952	38,650	75,071	16,844	5,035	8,702	263,224
1975	122,386	40,621	84,534	16,551	4,611	10,387	279,090
1976	131,603	41,409	90,769	16,963	5,216	12,101	298,060
1977	157,626	54,892	106,485	17,548	7,327	11,681	355,559
1978	180,988	59,952	120,967	18,376	5,285	13,993	399,561
1979	217,841	65,677	138,939	18,745	5,411	16,690	463,302
1980	244,069	64,600	157,803	24,329	6,389	19,922	517,112
1981	285,917	61,137	182,720	40,839	6,787	21,872	599,272
1982	297,744	49,207	201,498	36,311	7,991	25,015	617,766
1983	288,938	37,022	208,994	35,300	6,053	24,256	600,562
1984	298,415	56,893	239,376	37,361	6,010	28,382	666,486
1985	334,531	61,331	265,163	35,992	6,422	30,598	734,088
1986	348,959	63,143	283,901	32,919	6,958	33,275	769,215
1987	392,557	83,926	303,318	32,457	7,493	34,536	854,353
1988	401,181	94,508	334,335	35,227	7,594	36,393	909,303
1989	445,690	103,291	359,416	34,386	8,745	39,576	991,190
1990	466,884	93,507	380,047	35,345	11,500	44,688	1,031,969
1991	467,827	98,086	396,016	42,402	11,138	39,527	1,055,041
1992	475,964	100,270	413,689	45,569	11,143	44,588	1,091,279
1993	509,680	117,520	428,300	48,057	12,577	38,206	1,154,401
1994	543,055	140,385	461,475	55,225	15,225	43,215	1,258,627
1995	590,244	157,004	484,473	57,484	14,763	47,833	1,351,830
1996	656,417	171,824	509,414	54,014	17,189	44,197	1,453,062
1997	737,466	182,293	539,371	56,924	19,845	43,341	1,579,292
1998	828,586	188,677	571,831	57,673	24,076	50,890	1,721,798
1999	879,480	184,680	611,833	70,414	27,782	53,270	1,827,454
2000	1,004,462	207,289	652,852	68,865	29,010	62,720	2,025,198
2001	994,339	151,075	693,967	66,232	28,400	57,129	1,991,142
2002	858,345	148,044	700,760	66,989	26,507	52,504	1,853,149
2003	793,699	131,778	712,978	67,524	21,959	54,383	1,782,321
2004	808,959	189,371	733,407	69,855	24,831	53,703	1,880,126
2005	927,222	278,282	794,125	73,094	24,764	56,138	2,153,625
2006	1,043,908	353,915	837,821	73,961	27,877	69,394	2,406,876
2007	1,163,472	370,243	869,607	65,069	26,044	73,566	2,568,001
2008	1,145,747	304,346	900,155	67,334	28,844	77,573	2,523,999
2009	915,308	138,229	890,917	62,483	23,482	74,576	2,104,995

[1] Employment taxes comprise old-age and survivors insurance, disability insurance, hospital insurance, railroad
retirement, railroad social security equivalent account, employment insurance, employee share of Federal employees
retirement, and certain non-Federal employees retirement.

[2] Other receipts are primarily composed of [1] customs duties and fees, and [2] deposits of earnings by the Federal
Reserve system.

Source: Office of Management and Budget, *Historical Tables, Budget of the U.S. Government, Fiscal Year 2011*, and JCT calculations.

Table 11.–Federal Receipts by Source, As a Percentage of GDP, 1950-2009

Fiscal Year	Individual Income Tax	Corporate Tax	Employment[1] Taxes	Excise Taxes	Estate and Gift Taxes	Other[2] Receipts	Total
1950	5 8	3.8	1.6	2 8	0 3	0.2	14.4
1951	6 8	4.4	1.8	2.7	0 2	0.3	16.1
1952	8 0	6.1	1.8	2 5	0 2	0.3	19.0
1953	8 0	5.7	1.8	2.7	0 2	0.3	18.7
1954	7 8	5.6	1.9	2 6	0 2	0.3	18.5
1955	7 3	4.5	2.0	2 3	0 2	0.2	16.5
1956	7 5	4.9	2.2	2 3	0 3	0.3	17.5
1957	7 9	4.7	2.2	2 3	0 3	0.3	17.7
1958	7 5	4.4	2.4	2 3	0 3	0.3	17.3
1959	7 5	3.5	2.4	2 2	0 3	0.3	16.2
1960	7 8	4.1	2.8	2 3	0 3	0.4	17.8
1961	7 8	4.0	3.1	2 2	0.4	0.4	17.8
1962	8 0	3.6	3.0	2 2	0.4	0.3	17.6
1963	7 9	3.6	3.3	2 2	0.4	0.4	17.8
1964	7 6	3.7	3.4	2.1	0.4	0.4	17.6
1965	7.1	3.7	3.2	2.1	0.4	0.4	17.0
1966	7 3	4.0	3.4	1.7	0.4	0.5	17.3
1967	7 6	4.2	4.0	1.7	0.4	0.5	18.4
1968	7 9	3.3	3.9	1 6	0.4	0.5	17.6
1969	9 2	3.9	4.1	1 6	0.4	0.6	19.7
1970	8 9	3.2	4.4	1 6	0.4	0.6	19.0
1971	8 0	2.5	4.4	1 5	0 3	0.6	17.3
1972	8.1	2.7	4.5	1 3	0 5	0.6	17.6
1973	7 9	2.8	4.8	1 2	0.4	0.5	17.6
1974	8 3	2.7	5.2	1 2	0.4	0.6	18.3
1975	7 8	2.6	5.4	1.1	0 3	0.7	17.9
1976	7 6	2.4	5.2	1 0	0 3	0.7	17.1
1977	8 0	2.8	5.4	0 9	0.4	0.6	18.0
1978	8 2	2.7	5.5	0 8	0 2	0.6	18.0
1979	8.7	2.6	5.6	0.7	0 2	0.7	18.5
1980	9 0	2.4	5.8	0 9	0 2	0.7	19.0
1981	9.4	2.0	6.0	1 3	0 2	0.7	19.6
1982	9 2	1.5	6.3	1.1	0 2	0.8	19.2
1983	8.4	1.1	6.1	1 0	0 2	0.7	17.5
1984	7 8	1.5	6.2	1 0	0 2	0.7	17.3
1985	8.1	1.5	6.4	0 9	0 2	0.7	17.7
1986	7 9	1.4	6.4	0.7	0 2	0.8	17.5
1987	8.4	1.8	6.5	0.7	0 2	0.7	18.4
1988	8 0	1.9	6.7	0.7	0 2	0.7	18.2
1989	8 3	1.9	6.7	0 6	0 2	0.7	18.4
1990	8.1	1.6	6.6	0 6	0 2	0.8	18.0
1991	7 9	1.7	6.7	0.7	0 2	0.7	17.8
1992	7 6	1.6	6.6	0.7	0 2	0.7	17.5
1993	7.7	1.8	6.5	0.7	0 2	0.6	17.5
1994	7 8	2.0	6.6	0 8	0 2	0.6	18.0
1995	8 0	2.1	6.6	0 8	0 2	0.7	18.4
1996	8 5	2.2	6.6	0.7	0 2	0.6	18.8
1997	9 0	2.2	6.6	0.7	0 2	0.5	19.2
1998	9 6	2.2	6.6	0.7	0 3	0.6	19.9
1999	9 6	2.0	6.6	0 8	0 3	0.6	19.8
2000	10 2	2.1	6.6	0.7	0 3	0.6	20.6
2001	9.7	1.5	6.8	0 6	0 3	0.6	19.5
2002	8.1	1.4	6.6	0 6	0 3	0.5	17.6
2003	7 2	1.2	6.5	0 6	0 2	0.5	16.2
2004	6 9	1.6	6.3	0 6	0 2	0.5	16.1
2005	7 5	2.2	6.4	0 6	0 2	0.5	17.3
2006	7 9	2.7	6.3	0 6	0 2	0.5	18.2
2007	8.4	2.7	6.3	0 5	0 2	0.5	18.5
2008	7 9	2.1	6.2	0 5	0 2	0.5	17.5
2009	6.4	1.0	6.3	0.4	0 2	0.5	14.8
1950-2009 Avg.	8.0	2.8	5.0	1.3	0.3	0.5	17.9

[1] Employment taxes comprise old-age and survivors insurance, disability insurance, hospital insurance, railroad
retirement, railroad Social Security equivalent account, employment insurance, employee share of Federal employees
retirement, and certain non-Federal employees retirement.

[2] Other receipts are primarily composed of (1) customs duties and fees, and (2) deposits of earnings by the Federal
Reserve system.

Source: Office of Management and Budget, *Historical Tables, Budget of the U.S. Government, Fiscal Year 2011;*
Economic Report of the President, 2010, Table B-78 for fiscal year GDP Figures.

Table 12.–Federal Receipts by Source, As a Percentage of Total Revenues, 1950-2009

Fiscal Year	Individual Income Tax	Corporate Tax	Employment[1] Taxes	Excise Taxes	Estate and Gift Taxes	Other[2] Receipts
1950	39.9	26.5	11.0	19.1	1.8	1.7
1951	41.9	27.3	11.0	16 8	1.4	1.7
1952	42.2	32.1	9.7	13.4	1.2	1.3
1953	42.8	30.5	9.8	14 2	1.3	1.4
1954	42.4	30.3	10.3	14 3	1.3	1.4
1955	43.9	27.3	12.0	14 0	1.4	1.4
1956	43.2	28.0	12.5	13 3	1.6	1.5
1957	44.5	26.5	12.5	13 2	1.7	1.6
1958	43.6	25.2	14.1	13.4	1.7	2.0
1959	46.3	21.8	14.8	13 3	1.7	2.0
1960	44.0	23.2	15.9	12.6	1.7	2.5
1961	43.8	22.2	17.4	12.6	2.0	2.0
1962	45.7	20.6	17.1	12.6	2.0	2.0
1963	44.7	20.3	18.6	12.4	2.0	2.1
1964	43.2	20.9	19.5	12 2	2.1	2.1
1965	41.8	21.8	19.0	12 5	2.3	2.6
1966	42.4	23.0	19.5	10 0	2.3	2.8
1967	41.3	22.8	21.9	9 2	2.0	2.7
1968	44.9	18.7	22.2	9 2	2.0	3.0
1969	46.7	19.6	20.9	8.1	1.9	2.8
1970	46.9	17.0	23.0	8.1	1.9	3.0
1971	46.1	14.3	25.3	8 9	2.0	3.4
1972	45.7	15.5	25.4	7 5	2.6	3.3
1973	44.7	15.7	27.3	7 0	2.1	3.1
1974	45.2	14.7	28.5	6.4	1.9	3.3
1975	43.9	14.6	30.3	5 9	1.7	3.7
1976	44.2	13.9	30.5	5.7	1.7	4.1
1977	44.3	15.4	29.9	4 9	2.1	3.3
1978	45.3	15.0	30.3	4.6	1.3	3.5
1979	47.0	14.2	30.0	4 0	1.2	3.6
1980	47.2	12.5	30.5	4.7	1.2	3.9
1981	47.7	10.2	30.5	6 8	1.1	3.6
1982	48.2	8.0	32.6	5 9	1.3	4.0
1983	48.1	6.2	34.8	5 9	1.0	4.0
1984	44.8	8.5	35.9	5.6	0.9	4.3
1985	45.6	8.4	36.1	4 9	0.9	4.2
1986	45.4	8.2	36.9	4 3	0.9	4.3
1987	46.0	9.8	35.5	3 8	0.9	4.0
1988	44.1	10.4	36.8	3 9	0.8	4.0
1989	45.0	10.4	36.3	3 5	0.9	4.0
1990	45.2	9.1	36.8	3.4	1.1	4.3
1991	44.3	9.3	37.5	4 0	1.1	3.7
1992	43.6	9.2	37.9	4 2	1.0	4.1
1993	44.2	10.2	37.1	4 2	1.1	3.3
1994	43.1	11.2	36.7	4.4	1.2	3.4
1995	43.7	11.6	35.8	4 3	1.1	3.5
1996	45.2	11.8	35.1	3.7	1.2	3.0
1997	46.7	11.5	34.2	3.6	1.3	2.7
1998	48.1	11.0	33.2	3 3	1.4	3.0
1999	48.1	10.1	33.5	3 9	1.5	2.9
2000	49.6	10.2	32.2	3.4	1.4	3.1
2001	49.9	7.6	34.9	3 3	1.4	2.9
2002	46.3	8.0	37.8	3.6	1.4	2.8
2003	44.5	7.4	40.0	3 8	1.2	3.1
2004	43.0	10.1	39.0	3.7	1.3	2.9
2005	43.1	12.9	36.9	3.4	1.1	2.6
2006	43.4	14.7	34.8	3.1	1.2	2.9
2007	45.3	14.4	33.9	2 5	1.0	2.9
2008	45.4	12.1	35.7	2.7	1.1	3.1
2009	43.5	6.6	42.3	3 0	1.1	3.5
1950-2009 Avg.	44.8	15.7	27.7	7.3	1.5	3.0

[1] Employment taxes comprise old-age and survivors insurance, disability insurance, hospital insurance, railroad retirement, railroad Social Security equivalent account, employment insurance, employee share of Federal employees retirement, and certain non-Federal employees retirement.

[2] Other receipts are primarily composed of (1) customs duties and fees, and (2) deposits of earnings by the Federal Reserve system.

Source: Office of Management and Budget, *Historical Tables, Budget of the U.S. Government, Fiscal Year 2011.*

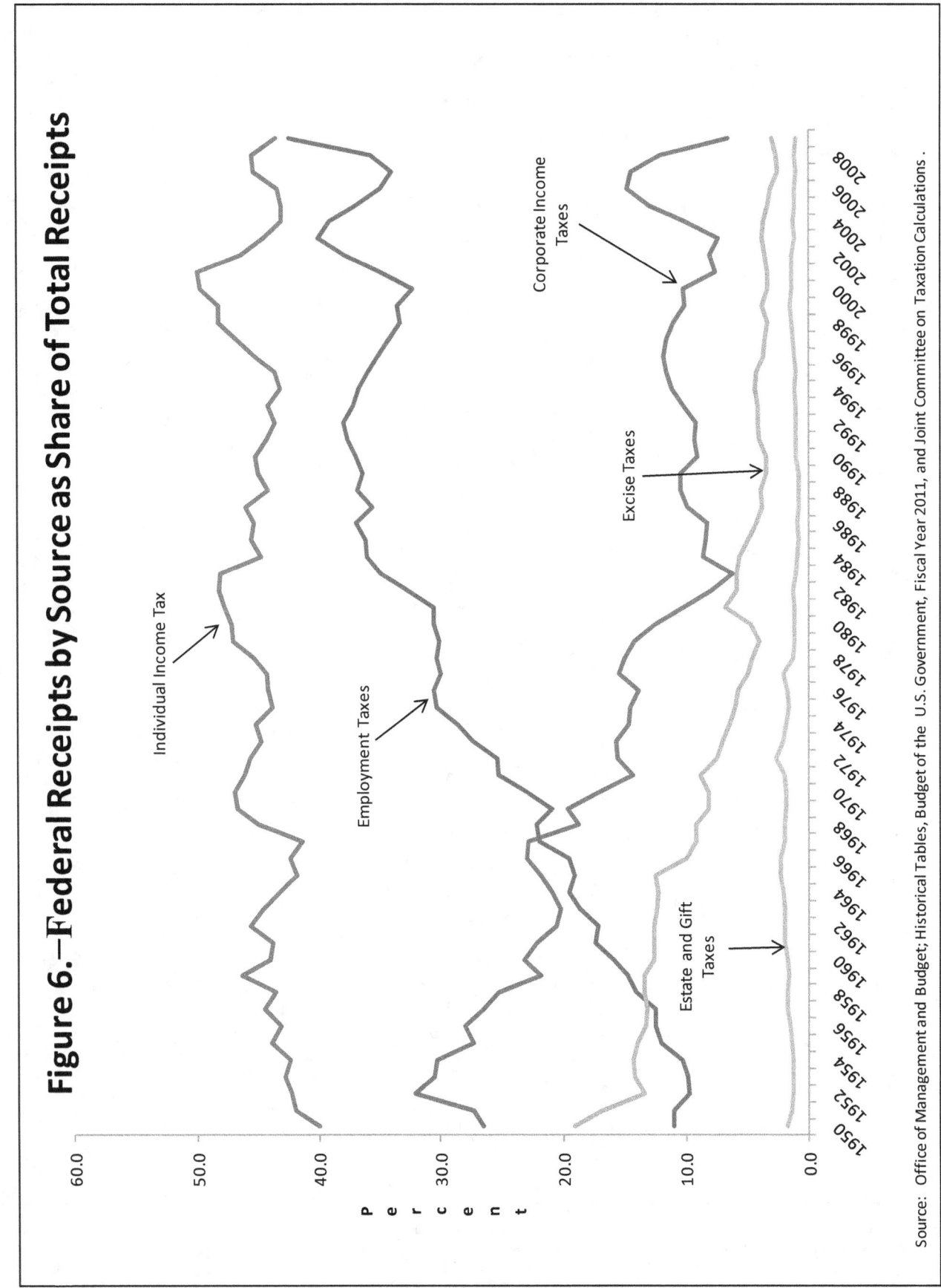

Figure 6.—Federal Receipts by Source as Share of Total Receipts

Individual Income Tax

Employment Taxes

Corporate Income Taxes

Excise Taxes

Estate and Gift Taxes

Percent

60.0 50.0 40.0 30.0 20.0 10.0 0.0

1950 1952 1954 1956 1958 1960 1962 1964 1966 1968 1970 1972 1974 1976 1978 1980 1982 1984 1986 1988 1990 1992 1994 1996 1998 2000 2002 2004 2006 2008

Source: Office of Management and Budget; Historical Tables, Budget of the U.S. Government, Fiscal Year 2011, and Joint Committee on Taxation Calculations .

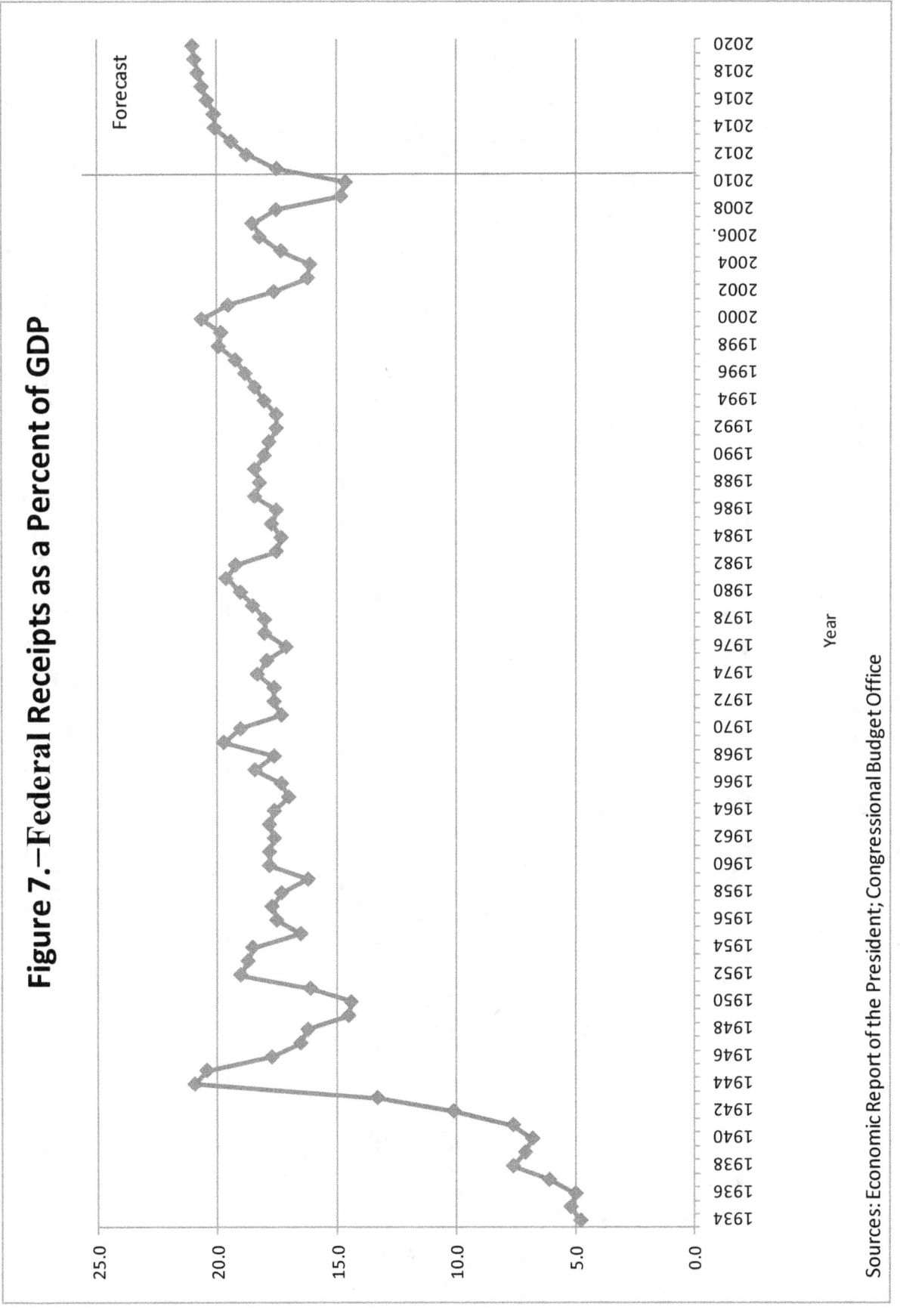

Figure 7.—Federal Receipts as a Percent of GDP

Year

Sources: Economic Report of the President; Congressional Budget Office

70

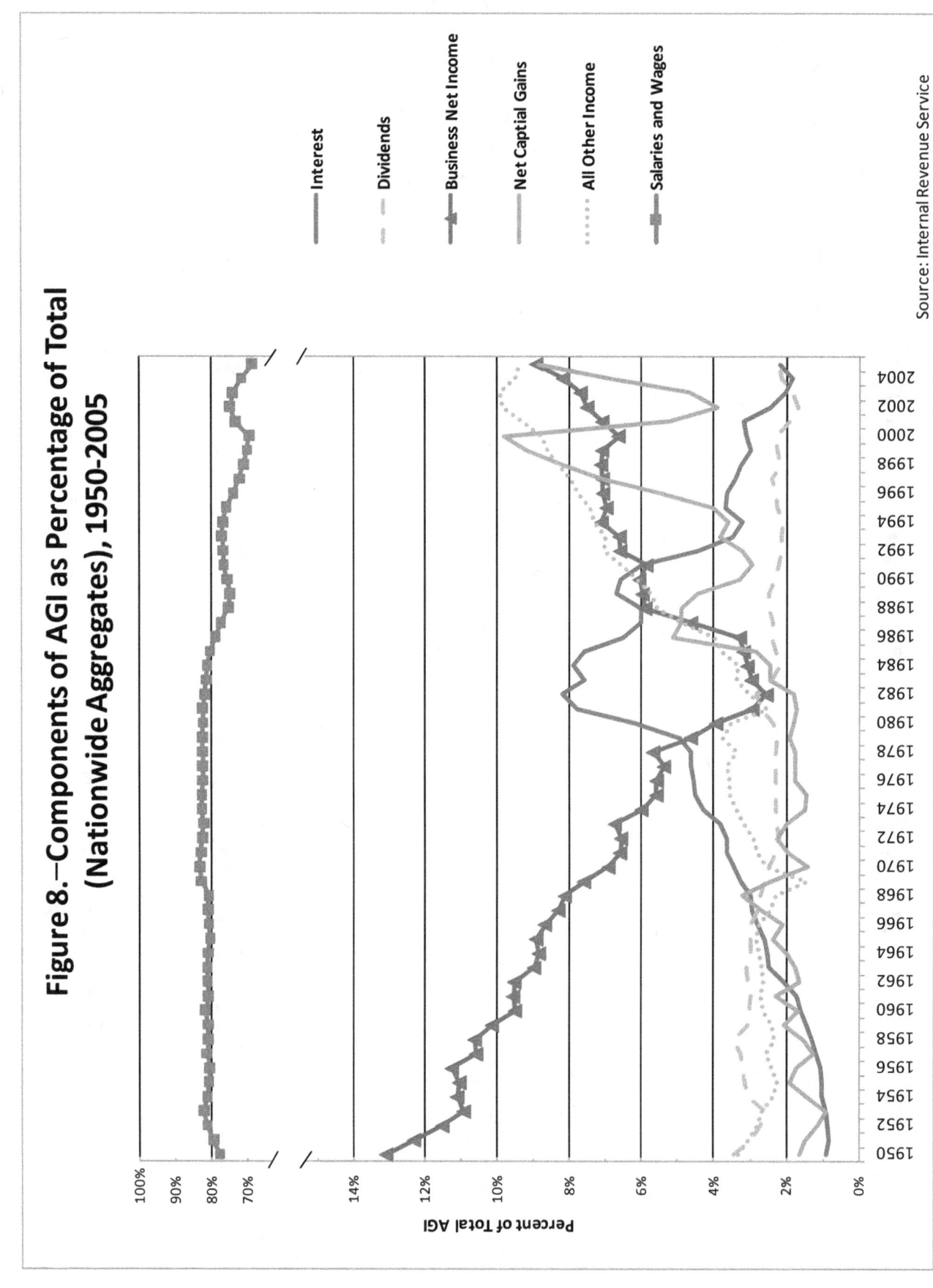

Figure 8.–Components of AGI as Percentage of Total (Nationwide Aggregates), 1950-2005

Legend:
- Interest
- Dividends
- Business Net Income
- Net Captial Gains
- All Other Income
- Salaries and Wages

Source: Internal Revenue Service

Figure 9.—Components of AGI, Constant 2005 Dollars

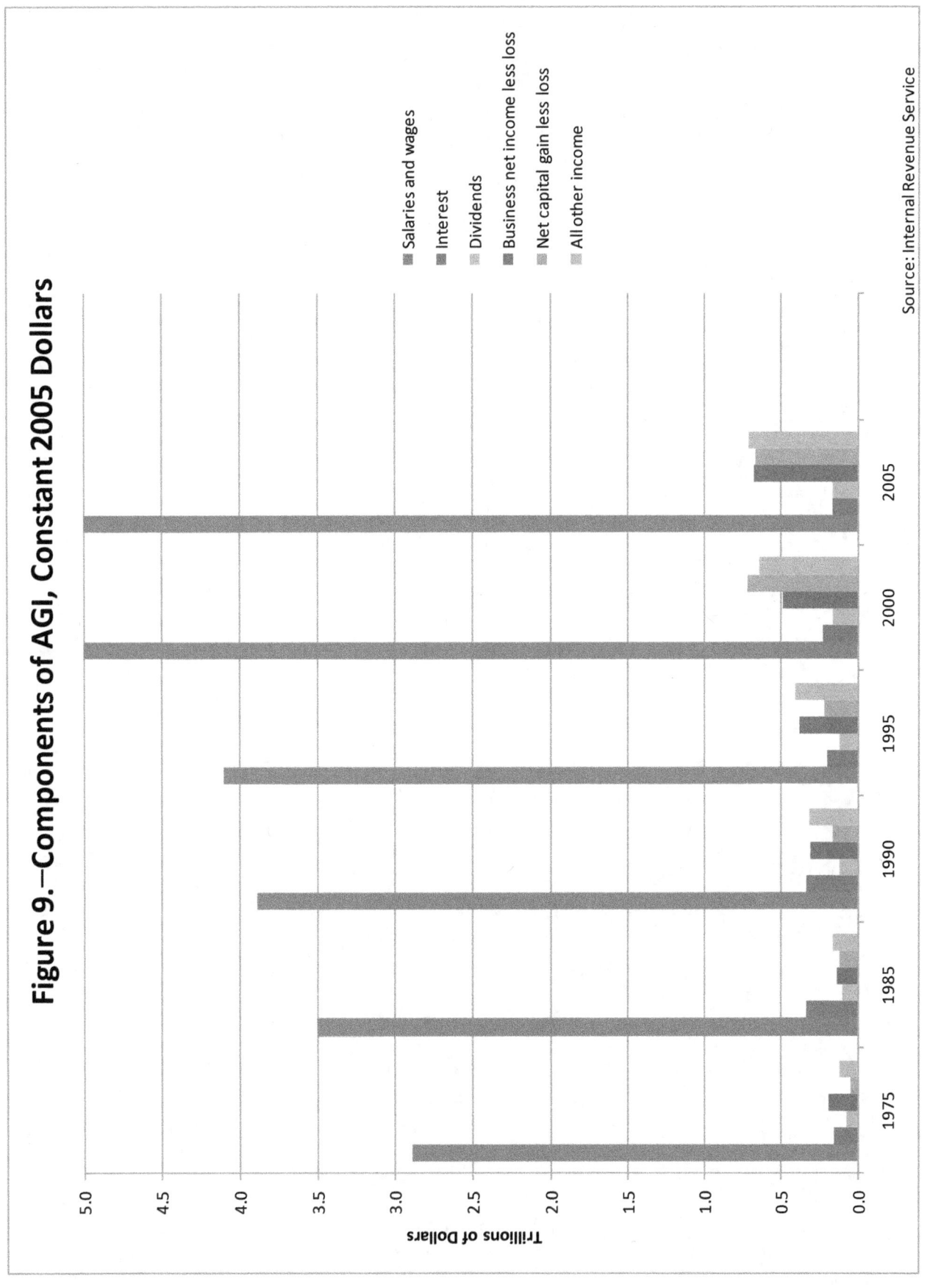

Source: Internal Revenue Service